THE SECRET

A Musical P.

Based upon the novel by
Frances Hodgson Burnett

Music, musical scores and lyrics by
Sharon Burgett

Additional lyrics by **Diana Matterson,
Sue Beckwith-Smith** and **Jim Crabtree**

Book by **Jim Crabtree**

Based in part on additional material by
Diana Matterson and **Sue Beckwith-Smith**

Orchestrations and vocal arrangements by
Larry Wilcox

Additional arrangements and orchestrations by
Ann Crabtree

Dramatic Publishing
Woodstock, Illinois • London, England • Melbourne, Australia

THE SECRET GARDEN was first produced on April 29, 1994 in Crossville, Tennessee, at the Cumberland County Playhouse under the supervision of Jim Crabtree, Producing Director. The production included the following artists:

MARY LENNOX .... *Katherine Hill, Chelsea Patterson*
MRS. MEDLOCK .... *Carol Irvin*
ARCHIBALD CRAVEN .... *Terry Schwab*
MARTHA SOWERBY .... *Weslie Webster*
BEN WEATHERSTAFF .... *Ty Stover*
DOCTOR CRAVEN .... *Jack Irvin*
DICKON SOWERBY .... *Daniel Roberts*
COLIN CRAVEN .... *Nathaniel Flatt, Justin McCormic*

Director .... *Abigail Crabtree*
Musical Director .... *Ann Crabtree*
Choreographer .... *Michele Franciosa*
Set Design .... *Joe Varga*
Costume Design .... *Renee Garrett Luttrell*
Lighting Design .... *Steve Woods*
Sound Design .... *Howard Rose*
Technical Director .... *John Partyka*
Production Stage Manager .... *Richard Blanton*
Properties .... *Tracy Simpson*

THE SECRET GARDEN

A Musical Play in Two Acts
For 3 Men, 3 Women, 1 Boy, 1 Girl, 3 Puppet Characters
and Chorus

CHARACTERS

MARY LENNOX .... 10 years old
MRS. MEDLOCK .... the housekeeper, middle-aged
ARCHIBALD CRAVEN ..... master of the Manor, Mary's
guardian
MARTHA SOWERBY ....a housemaid, in her 20s
BEN WEATHERSTAFF .... gardener of Misselthwaite
DOCTOR CRAVEN ...... Mr. Craven's cousin and Colin's
doctor
DICKON SOWERBY .... Martha's brother, about 15
COLIN CRAVEN .... Mary's cousin, 10 years old

and...
Narrator, Priest, His Wife, Their Children (Basil & Angela),
Altar Boys, Passengers, Crew, Other Ship Travelers,
Mourners, Portrait People (including Lilian, Children),
Gardeners, Servants, Robin, Fox, Crow, Squirrels

Production Notes

If a smaller cast is required, all of the main characters (except Mary) can double as ensemble for the opening sequences (I,1) underdressing costumes for I,2. Though a strong choral sound is a plus, portrait people and portrait children can be reduced in number or eliminated, and Medlock, Dr. Craven, Martha and Ben can sing "servant" sections, possibly with Dickon doubling as a servant. It is nice if Lilian is a dancer, and her presence adds mystery and poignancy, but she could also be cut.

The puppet characters could also be played by children, though it is nice for them to be smaller and very different from Mary. In the original production a combination of hand puppets and rod puppets were used. Fox and Squirrel(s) were hand puppets, Crow and Robin were rod puppets. The Gazebo, garden walls and Colin's bed were designed to conceal puppet operators. The Crow, if he caws loudly and chases Medlock via a rod puppet operated from under the bed, can be very funny.

ACT ONE

SCENE ONE

(MUSIC #1: "OVERTURE")

SETTING: *The front curtain is a scrim depicting a tangle of giant vines and branches around its border. They are still brown with winter's chill, and buds are just beginning to peek out in specks of color. Seen through the vines and branches are the looming walls of Misselthwaite Manor, and this scrim drop can therefore be used later as the setting for a location outside the Manor, on the grounds, near the Secret Garden. On the scrim is projected "The Secret Garden." When the overture concludes, the house lights fade, and we hear a mournful Indian melody, on solo oboe.*

Behind the scrim, partway U, a large map of British colonial India is revealed, and a group of INDIAN SERVANTS is seen, plus two Anglican ALTAR BOYS appear and a CLERGYMAN in cassock and surplice. Two caskets are brought on, one from each side, to C, and the PRIEST and ALTAR BOYS move to C. BRITISH CITIZENS in mourning garb complete the picture. The music segues to an Anglican hymn of mourning.

(MUSIC #2: "OPENING")

PRIEST.
> INTO THY HANDS, OH LORD, WE COMMEND
> THY SPIRITS...

PEOPLE *(repeating).*
> **INTO THY HANDS, OH LORD, WE COMMEND
> THY SPIRIT**

(The chord sustains as a woman's voice is heard, and the music softens. THE NARRATOR's words are projected where the title was before. The projections have illustrated letters beginning them, as in a beautiful children's book.)

SLIDE: When Mary Lennox...

NARRATOR. When Mary Lennox was ten years old, she was left alone.

(MARY is seen, DRC, facing front. The caskets are U, behind her. She stands alone, in white with black accessories, and a suitcase, as if ready for a journey.)

PEOPLE.
> **THOU HAST REDEEMED US, OH LORD THOU
> GOD OF TRUTH, WE COMMEND THEIR
> SPIRIT...**

(They continue humming the chant, under. Cue for Narration. The key phrases of the NARRATOR's text are projected in various places on the scrim.)

SLIDE: Mary was orphaned...

NARRATOR. Mary was orphaned when the cholera swept India, taking her parents. But really, she had always been alone.

PEOPLE.
> **GLORY BE TO THE FATHER, AND TO THE SON,**
> **AND TO THE HOLY GHOST...**
> *(Humming continues under.)*

(Father's casket moves in as there is a change of light D and "Father" is seen to MARY's right in conversation with men. She turns to him but he doesn't notice.)

SLIDE: Mary's father...

NARRATOR. Mary's father was always busy with the English government...

(Mother's casket in as "mother" appears to MARY's left with an admirer.)

SLIDE: And her mother...

NARRATOR. And her mother was a great beauty who cared only to go to parties and amuse herself. She had not wanted a little girl at all, and handed Mary over to an ayah—an Indian nanny. *(MARY has approached "mother" and been shoo'd to the ayah, as "mother" exits. MARY walks away from ayah and back to C.)*

PRIEST & PEOPLE.
> **GLORY BE TO THE FATHER,**
> **AND TO THE SON, AND TO THE HOLY GHOST...**
> *(The voices fade away. The funeral ends, the scrim flies, MARY is left alone.)*

(Another CLERGYMAN and his WIFE approach MARY.)

NARRATOR. She was ignored by her parents and spoiled by her ayah, so by the time her parents died, Mary Lennox was as tyrannical and selfish a little pig as ever existed. *(MARY stomps, walks away from CLERGYMAN, who pursues, and is pursued by his WIFE and CHILDREN.)* And she knew that she was NOT going to stay at the clergyman's house where she was taken at first. *(She shakes her head, and the CLERGYMAN and his WIFE exit, leaving her with the CHILDREN.)*

MARY *(to the CHILDREN)*. Go away! I don't want you. Go AWAY!

BASIL *(teasing her, the other CHILDREN joining, chanting)*.
    MISTRESS MARY, QUITE CONTRARY
    HOW DOES YOUR GARDEN GROW?
    WITH SILVER BELLS, AND COCKLE SHELLS
    AND MARIGOLDS ALL IN A ROW
    (Repeat, perhaps with more melody. The other CHILDREN laugh, and MARY runs away in frustration.)
    You are going to be sent home! At the end of the week! To live with your uncle! And we're glad of it!

MARY. I'm glad of it too! *(Turns and walks away. Stops. To herself.)* Where IS home?

ANGELA *(telling a spooky story)*. I heard father and mother talking about him. He lives in England, where it rains all the time, and the sun never shines like here in India! He lives in a great, big, desolate old house in the country and no one goes near him! He's a hunchback, and he's horrid!

(As the CHILDREN sing and taunt MARY again they chase her about, and are joined by the MINISTER and his WIFE, plus other TRAVELERS heading for England, as the stage transforms into dockside and then just as rapidly into a

*masted sailing vessel with one or two large sails which
drop from above. The sails are held in place by the PAS-
SENGERS and CREW.)*

CHILDREN.
>MISTRESS MARY, QUITE CONTRARY
>HOW DOES YOUR GARDEN GROW
>WHERE THE HUNCHBACK DWELLS WITH HIS
> MAGIC SPELLS
>IN A HOUSE WHERE NONE WILL GO

CHILDREN & ENSEMBLE.
>MISTRESS MARY, BEST BE WARY
>WHERE YOU ARE BOUND TO GO
>TO ENGLAND'S SHORES AND YORKSHIRE
> MOORS
>WHERE THERE'S NAUGHT BUT RAIN AND
> SNOW!

>MISTRESS MARY, DARK AND SCARY'S
>THE PLACE WHERE YOU'RE BOUND TO GO
>IT'S A GREAT UNKNOWN—
>YOU'LL BE ALL ALONE—
>IN A HOUSE WHERE NO 'NE WILL GO—
*(A sail falls from above or is lifted up and the ship is un-
derway.)*
>SAILING OFF TO ENGLAND GREEN,
>ENGLAND GREY
>SAYING OUR GOODBYES
>STARTING OUR NEW LIVES TODAY

>AND WHEN WE CLOSE OUR EYES AND BOW
> OUR HEADS

IT'S TO OUR GOD WE PRAY
HE WILL GODSPEED US
HE WILL GODSPEED US

***Begin cut here for one-act edition.

SAILING THOUGH THE LONELY NIGHT,
STORMY DAY
SAILING WITH THE WINDS,
SAILING ON THE MIGHTY WAVES
AND WHEN AN ENDLESS SEA
LEADS US TO FEEL
WE'LL NEVER FIND THE WAY
HE WILL GODSPEED US
HE WILL GODSPEED US

MARY (*moving from the others*).
WHERE IS HOME
I KEEP WOND'RING WHERE IS HOME?
IS THERE A PLACE I WON'T BE SO ALONE—

IF I COULD FLY
THROUGH A MAGIC CARPET SKY
I'D FLY WHERE I WOULD NEVER EVER BE
SO ALONE
SO ALONE

***Continue here for one-act edition.

MARY, PASSENGERS & CREW.
SAILING OFF TO ENGLAND GREEN,
ENGLAND GREY

SAYING OUR GOODBYES
STARTING OUR NEW LIVES TODAY

AND WHEN WE CLOSE OUR EYES AND BOW
   OUR HEADS
AND THANK THEE FOR THIS DAY
HE WILL GODSPEED US
HE WILL GODSPEED US
WE'LL SAIL TO A NEW LIFE
NEW DAY—

(The number ends, and the PASSENGERS and CREW transform the stage. We see MARY passed to two nuns as thunder is heard powerfully and lightning pierces the darkness, and the setting changes to the Great Hall of Misselthwaite Manor.)

(MUSIC #2A: "OPENING PLAYOFF")

***For one-act edition, please use the following lyrics for the last verse.

SAILING OFF TO ENGLAND GREEN, ENGLAND
   GREY
SAILING ON THE WINDS
SAILING ON THE MIGHTY WAVES

AND WHEN AN ENDLESS SEA LEADS US TO
   FEEL
WE'LL NEVER FIND THE WAY
HE WILL GODSPEED US
WE'LL SAIL TO A NEW LIFE
NEW DAY!

SCENE TWO

SETTING: *The Great Hall, Misselthwaite Manor. A stormy night. The Great Hall suggests an Entry area and a Parlor and is used for arrivals and "at home" scenes. The Hall, like the rest of the Manor, is populated by figures in portraits, with frames of every size, plus suits of armor standing guard. The portraits include some actors behind frames which are part of the set, and some frames actually held by the person in the portrait. At first, in the spooky light, the fact that some "portraits" are alive should not be evident. This convention will continue during the show—black attired servants will "become" the portraits on the walls, by doffing an apron, donning an archaic hat, and stepping into or holding up a gilded frame. On this stormy night our first impression of the Manor lives up to its spooky reputation. It is clearly a house with ghosts. Perhaps during the transition a projection [with illustrated first letter] tells us where we are:*

MISSELTHWAITE MANOR, Yorkshire, England

As the transition completes, two MAIDS are seen, and a loud crack of thunder and lightning starts them squealing and giggling. MRS. MEDLOCK enters briskly, the MAIDS instantly recover their composure, curtsy to her and exit. MEDLOCK leans to read something on the desk as a bent, shadowy figure enters on the stairs, then speaks.

ARCHIE. Good evening, Mrs. Medlock.

MEDLOCK *(startled, polishing again)*. Oh! Mr. Craven, I was—

ARCHIE *(moving into the light)*. I've had a telegram from London. Miss Lennox has arrived from Bombay. She will be on the 10 p.m. train from Kings Cross tonight.

MEDLOCK. Tonight?

ARCHIE. You'll see that rooms are made ready for her, Mrs. Medlock.

MEDLOCK. I'll have the old nurseries in the West Tower opened up for her. Well away from...

ARCHIE *(quickly)*. Yes. Quite. You must ensure Miss Mary is confined to her rooms when she is not downstairs. She must not wander about the house at random.

MEDLOCK *(ingratiating)*. Understood, sir. It's not every orphan that's lucky enough to have an uncle willing to care for her.

ARCHIE. It's the least I can do for my dear Lilian. *(He turns toward one of the portraits, as it brightens.)* Now her only sister is gone, too.

MEDLOCK. God rest her soul.

ARCHIE. Make the girl as welcome as possible. Brighten up this dreary house if you can. *(Exits.)*

MEDLOCK *(claps hands, rings a bell, with a flourish)*. Staff to the Great Hall, please—to the Great Hall of Missel-thwaite Manor! *(As SERVANTS assemble...)*

(MUSIC #3: "ANY MINUTE NOW")

MEDLOCK *(sings)*.
>**THE CARRIAGE WILL BE COMIN'**
>**ANY MINUTE NOW!**
>**IS EVERYBODY READY?**
>**ANY MINUTE NOW!**

ENSEMBLE.
> **WE'VE MADE THIS DREARY HOUSE**
> **A BRIGHTER HOUSE TODAY**
> **IT'S SUCH A GLOOMY HOUSE**
> **FOR ANY CHILD TO STA-AA-AAY**

BEN.
> **I'VE CLIPPED THE HEDGES**
> **NEATLY IN A ROW**

SOLO MAN.
> **AND I'VE PRUNED THE ROSES**
> **SO THE BLOOMS WILL GROW**

ALL.
> **AND WE HAVE MOWED AND HOED**
> **THE WHOLE DAY LONG FOR SOMEONE WHOM**
> **WE KNOW IS**
> **COMIN' ANY, COMIN' ANY, COMIN' ANY,**
> **COMIN' ANY,**
> **ANY MINUTE NOW**
> *(Waltz tempo now.)*

MAIDS.
> **WE'VE POLISHED MAHOGANY, RUBBED UP**
> **THE OAK**
> **AND WE'VE SCRUBBED EACH STONE ON THE**
> **FLOOR**

MEN.
> **WITH ONE HUNDRED ROOMS WHO'S TO SAY**
> **IF WE'RE DONE**

ALL.

AND BESIDES, IN ONE MINUTE MORE
THERE'S A LITTLE GIRL COMIN'
A LITTLE GIRL COMIN'
A HOTHOUSE INDIAN PLANT
IN A DAMP ENGLISH WINTER IN YORKSHIRE
SHE'LL WISH SHE WERE ELSEWHERE
UNTIL SPRING PUSHES THROUGH

WHEN THE MOOR IS IN BLOOM
AND THE WORLD IS A ROOM
FULL OF BLUE SKIES AND BUTTERFLIES
IF SHE'LL CLOSE HER EYES
SHE'LL SEE IT TOO
SHE'LL SEE IT TOO

WOMEN.

WE'VE BRUSHED AWAY THE COBWEBS
AND CHASED AWAY THE GLOOM
LET'S HOPE OUR GIRL IS GIVEN
A CHEERFUL LITTLE ROOM

SHE'S GOING TO NEED SOMEONE
TO HUG HER WHEN SHE'S SAD
SOMEONE WHO'LL BE HER MUM
AND SPANK HER WHEN SHE'S BAD–BADD–BAD!

SEE THE CARRIAGE COMIN' (SEE IT COMIN'
NOW)
SHE'LL BE HERE AT LAST (SHE'LL BE HERE
AT LAST)
TO BRIGHTEN UP OUR FUTURE
AND SWEEP AWAY THE PAST

AND AFTER ALL THESE YEARS
IMAGINE HEARING LAUGHTER ONCE AGAIN
SHE'S GOING TO NEED A FAMILY
GOING TO NEED A FAMILY
ANY MINUTE
THE CARRIAGE WILL BE COMIN', COMIN',
   COMIN', COMIN', COMIN', COMIN'
ANY MINUTE NOW!

(During the number, the faces in the portraits participate. At the end of the song, MEDLOCK claps her hands, and moves to the door. The SERVANTS line up. MARY LENNOX enters, and she and MEDLOCK come face to face.)

MARY. Who are you?

MEDLOCK. I am Mrs. Medlock, the housekeeper. Your rooms are ready for you, Miss Mary, if you'd care to accompany me upstairs—

MARY. I would not care to—yet. Take my luggage up first. It's outside. I want to see my guardian.

MEDLOCK. Your uncle will no doubt send for you—when he wishes to see you.

MARY. If by my uncle you mean Mr. Archibald Craven, your employer, then kindly say so. My luggage, please! NOW! *(She exits, SERVANTS ushering her.)*

   (MUSIC #3A: "ANY MINUTE NOW"—Reprise)

ENSEMBLE.
   SHE'S GOING TO NEED A FAMILY
   GOING TO NEED A FAMILY
   ANY MINUTE

**THE CARRIAGE WILL BE COMIN', COMIN',
COMING COMIN', COMIN', COMIN'
ANY MINUTE NOW!** *(Direct seque.)*

(MUSIC #3B: "PERCUSSION/SOUND CUE")

(Transition, more thunder and lightning and darkness. Crying and wailing is heard, but it is indistinct, almost as if caused by the wind, at first. EIGHT CHILDREN with picture frames enter across D, in one, in a corridor of light. These are the PORTRAIT CHILDREN, and they will appear from time to time. They take places as if hanging on a corridor wall, across the stage. They are dressed in costumes of various archaic periods, the younger generation of the manor's adult portrait residents. MARY walks in, looks around, is very frightened, and runs offstage.)

(MUSIC #3C: "ANY MINUTE NOW"—Playoff)

SCENE THREE

SETTING: *Mary's Room, Misselthwaite Manor. The next morning. The walls are covered with tapestry with a forest scene embroidered on it.*

MARY is in bed, fretful, hugging a pillow when the lights come up. There is a knock, and she turns over, pretending to be asleep. MARTHA enters quietly then goes to the "window" on the fourth wall to open the drapes—and light streams in. MARY sits up.

MARY (*pointing out the window*). What is that?

MARTHA. That's the moor. Does tha' like it?

MARY (*determinedly contrary*). No. I hate it.

MARTHA. That's because tha'rt not used to it. But tha' will like it.

MARY. Do you?

MARTHA. Aye, that I do. I just love it. It's covered wi' growin' things. Eh! I wouldn't live away from th' moor for anythin'.

MARY. Are you going to be my servant?

MARTHA. I'm Mrs. Medlock's servant. And she's Mr. Craven's—but I'm to do the housemaid's work up here an' wait on you a bit. But you won't need much waitin' on.

MARY. Who is going to dress me?

MARTHA. Canna' tha' dress thyself?

MARY. No, I never did in my life. My ayah dressed me, of course.

MARTHA. Your what?

MARY. My ayah. My servant.

MARTHA. Well, it's time tha' should learn. It'll do thee good to wait on thyself a bit.

MARY (*with a maharajah's majesty*). It is different in India.

MARTHA. Eh! I can see it's different! I dare say it's because they all sit out in the hot sun too long. (*Pause.*) When I heard you was comin' from India I thought you'd have a red spot and bedclothes on your head!

MARY (*furious*). What! What? You thought I was a native. You—you daughter of a pig! (*Throws a pillow to the floor.*

(MUSIC #4: "I WILL DO NOTHING")

MARTHA. Who are you callin' names!? You needn't be so vexed. That's not the way for a young lady to talk!

MARTHA *(sings).*

> GET QUICKLY OUT OF BED AND LET ME LOOK
>   AT THEE
> FROM HERE THOU LOOKS A SKINNY LITTLE
>   MITE TO ME
> I'VE HAD ABOUT AS MUCH AS I CAN TAKE
>   FROM THEE
> AND DO NOT THINK I WOULDN'T TAKE ME
>   HAND TO THEE!

MARY *(lounging back royally).*

> JUST BRING MY CLOTHES, I WISH TO DRESS
> AND DON'T YOU THINK IT'S TIME YOU LEARN
>   TO CHATTER LESS?
> FOR I CAN DO NOTHING, MOST DEFINITELY
>   NOTHING,
> I'M BRILLIANT AT NOTHING AND SADLY FEEL
>   NOTHING FOR YOU

MARTHA.

> SO YOU WILL DO NOTHING, MOST
>   DEFINITELY NOTHING,
> THERE'S CERTAINLY, DEFINITELY
>   SOMETHING THE MATTER WITH YOU
> I TELL YOU HERE RIGHT NOW, YOU'RE GOING
>   TO FIND SOMEHOW,
> THERE'RE LOTS OF LITTLE THINGS YOU'LL
>   HAVE TO LEARN TO DO
> SO LET ME MAKE IT CLEAR, THAT MY
>   POSITION HERE
> IS JUST TO HELP AND NOT TO BE A SLAVE TO
>   YOU!

MARY.
> WHO DO YOU THINK YOU'RE TALKING TO?
> NOW GET ME DRESSED AT ONCE AS YOU'RE
>   SUPPOSED TO DO
>
> FOR I WILL DO NOTHING,

MARTHA.
> MOST DEFINITELY NOTHING?

MARY.
> I'M BRILLIANT AT NOTHING

MARTHA.
> MOST CERTAINLY NOTHING

MARY.
> I ALWAYS NEED SOMEONE AND

BOTH.
> SOMEONE IS DEF'NITELY YOU.

MARY
> WELL, I KNOW I REALLY COULD, THO
> I DON'T SEE WHY I SHOULD,
> YOU'RE JUST A SERVANT, YOU MUST DO AS
>   YOU ARE TOLD

MARTHA.
> I'D NEVER DO AS I WAS TOLD BY ANY
>   CHEEKY TEN-YEAR-OLD

WHY I WOULD RATHER SCRUB THE TUBS,
RATHER SCRUB THE TUBS, RATHER SCRUB
THE TUBS
THAN GIVE A HAND TO YOU

MARY.

THIS WAIST IS MUCH TOO TIGHT, IT'S
UNDERNEATH MY CHIN
WHAT ARE THESE BUTTONS FOR, MY ARM
JUST WON'T GO IN
THESE STOCKINGS ARE TOO WIDE, MY LEGS
ARE MUCH TOO THIN
CAN'T YOU SEE THE DREADFUL TANGLED
MESS I'M IN?

MARTHA.

YOU THINK THAT LIFE'S A GAME TO PLAY
IT'S TIME YOU KNEW THAT TWO CAN PLAY
THE SAME GAME TOO!
YOUR MANNERS ARE CHILLING, I'D NEVER BE
WILLING
TO DRESS YOU OR HELP YOU TO BUTTON IT,
BUCKLE IT,
SNAP IT OR TUCK IT OR LACE IT OR TIE IN A
BOW, SO
I WILL DO NOTHING

MARY.

AND I CAN DO NOTHING

MARTHA.

DECIDEDLY NOTHING

MARY.
 INCAPABLY NOTHING

MARTHA.
 WELL, POSSIBLY NOTHING

MARY.
 WELL, PRACTICALLY NOTHING

MARTHA.
 THAT'S SOMETHING FOR NOTHING

BOTH.
 **I WILL DO NOTHING
 NO NOTHING, NO NOTHING
 NO NOTHING, NO NOTHING FOR YOU!**

(At end MARY is wildly disheveled. MEDLOCK enters.)

MEDLOCK. What DO you think you're doing, Martha? Why
 is this child got up like a scarecrow!

MARTHA *(not wanting to tattle)*. She...She...

MARY. I'm not used to dressing myself.

MEDLOCK. I can see that. Now pay attention, Miss Mary.
 Doctor Craven is coming to examine you this afternoon,
 after which you are to report for tea with your guardian in
 the Hall. Is that clear?

MARY. Doctor Craven?

MEDLOCK. The doctor is your guardian Mr. Craven's
 cousin. *(To MARTHA.)* See to it Miss Mary is washed and
 tidy by three o'clock.

MARTHA. Very good, Mrs. Medlock.

MEDLOCK. And remember that she is not to wander about the house.

MARTHA. Yes, mum.

MARY. It's going to be like prison here if I'm not allowed into any other rooms.

MARTHA. Well, then tha' will just go outside.

MARY. Outside? On the moor? I'd get lost.

MARTHA. Lost? When my mum sends my brothers and sisters, big and small, out to the moor to tumble about? My brother Dickon, he's fourteen, and he's got a wild pony he found on the moor. You wrap up warm and run out and play, you. It'll do you good.

MARY. Who will go with me?

MARTHA (*getting MARY's coat and helping her with it*). You'll go by yourself. My brother Dickon goes off on the moor by himself for hours. That's how he found the pony. He's got birds as comes and eats out o' his hand. (*Pointing out the window on the fourth wall.*) If tha' goes 'round that way tha'll come to the gardens. (*Pause.*) One o' the gardens is locked up. No one has been in it for ten years.

MARY. Why?

MARTHA (*sharing a secret*). Mr. Craven had it shut when his wife died so sudden. It was her garden. He locked the door and dug a hole and buried the key! Mr. Craven still mourns her. After all these years.

MARY. How did she die? (*A bell clangs loudly.*) What's that?

MARTHA. Mrs. Medlock's bell. We call it the Cow-Bell. Time for household prayers, but you're excused this morning. (*Suddenly, in the distance comes the sound of a child crying out, borne on the wind.*)

MARY. Listen! Listen—that sound—

MARTHA. It's the wind blowing over the moor, Miss Mary.

MARY. It sounds like...someone crying out...(*The sound again, fainter.*) There! Can you hear it?

MARTHA. That'll be Elsie, the scullery maid. She's had the toothache all week.

(Thunder echoes, the lights fade, as MARTHA exits and MARY listens to the cry once more. We move to the Great Hall as the SERVANTS sing household prayers.)

(MUSIC #5: "PRAISE GOD FROM WHOM ALL BLESSINGS FLOW")

SERVANTS.

**PRAISE GOD FROM WHOM ALL BLESSINGS FLOW,
PRAISE HIM ALL CREATURES HERE BELOW
PRAISE HIM ABOVE YE HEAVENLY HOST
PRAISE FATHER, SON, AND HOLY GHOST. AMEN.**

SCENE FOUR

SETTING: *The Great Hall. This scene is a direct vista segue from Scene 3; the doxology still rings in our ears, as the SERVANTS scurry away.*

A MAID brings DOCTOR CRAVEN to MRS. MEDLOCK.

ELSIE. Doctor Craven to see Mr. Craven and Miss Mary, mum.

MEDLOCK. Thank you, Elsie. I shall escort the doctor. *(ELSIE departs. CRAVEN and MEDLOCK wait a beat, look about them furtively, then CRAVEN kisses MEDLOCK's hand. She squeals as he kisses up the arm to her inner elbow.)*

MEDLOCK *(breaking the clinch).* Archie's gone for a ride. The girl is outside somewhere.

CRAVEN. What is she like? *(Stalking her.)*

MEDLOCK. A tiresome, spoilt child with a will of her own. Pale, skinny and sharp as a pikestaff. *(She pokes a finger in his ribs.)*

CRAVEN. You must keep then apart, Marion, lest she begin to console him.

MEDLOCK. Naturally.

(They break apart furtively as a MAID brings tea.)

CRAVEN. If I could only persuade Archie to go away, abroad somewhere, for a time. I've told him he should leave this unhappy place with its bitter memories—but he refuses.

MEDLOCK *(flirting with him).* If you insist too often, Richard, he may become suspicious, and that would interfere with OUR plans for Misselthwaite...

CRAVEN. Ah, what a mistress of the Manor you will be...*(He takes her hand and kisses along her arm. She laughs and squeals again.)*

MEDLOCK. Shh! We dare not speak it. We must maintain his trust...and WAIT! *(Sings.)*

(MUSIC #6: " WISHFUL THINKING")

**YOU WITH YOUR BEDSIDE MANNER
AND I IN MY USUAL COMPETENT, TOLERANT
   WAY—
WHO WOULD EVER SAY
OUR INTENTIONS, THO' CURIOUS
WERE MEANT TO BE SPURIOUS
AND JUST SLIGHTLY INJURIOUS**

CRAVEN.

> QUITE RIGHT, YOU COULD SAY, IN A MANNER
> OF SPEAKING
> THERE'S SOMETHING AFOOT IN THIS HOUSE
> WHICH MIGHT SLIGHTLY IMPLY, IN A
> MANNER OF SPEAKING
> THE CAT'S JUST BEEN PUT WITH THE MOUSE!

MEDLOCK.

> SO LITTLE TIME, SO MUCH TO DO,
> IS IT A CRIME, WISHFUL THINKING, WITH YOU?

CRAVEN.

> THE CRYSTAL CHANDELIERS, DECANTERS,
> CRESTED PLATES, MY DEAR

MEDLOCK.

> THE WALNUT SECRETAIRE, THOSE GEORGIAN
> CHAIRS, A BEAUVAIS TAPIS TOO

CRAVEN.

> A CELLAR STACKED WITH RACKS OF
> VINTAGE PORT, SOME CLARET ROUGE

MEDLOCK.

> AND CUPBOARDS BRIMMING FULL WITH
> LINENS, LACE AND DAMASK TABLE CLOTHS—

CRAVEN.

> THE SILVER MONOGRAMMED AND
> HALLMARKED—
> *(Spoken.)* Sixteen—

MEDLOCK.
>QUEEN ANNE—

CRAVEN.
>—NINETY-TWO!

MEDLOCK.
>SO LITTLE TIME!

CRAVEN.
>SO MUCH TO DO!

BOTH.
>IS IT A CRIME, WISHFUL THINKING, WITH YOU...

(They break apart again, hiding their flirtation, as the SERVANTS enter.)

MEN.
>TOO MANY ROOMS FOR JUST ONE MAN TO USE
>TOO MANY BUCKETS OF COAL

WOMEN.
>TOO MANY COBWEBS THEY'D NEVER EXCUSE

ALL.
>BETTER WATCH IT WHEN MEDLOCK
>>PATROLS—
>
>SO LITTLE TIME
>SO MUCH TO DO
>IS IT A CRIME TO MISS A CORNER OR TWO?

> THE GRAND PIANO IN THE PARLOR HAS GOT
>   EIGHTY-EIGHT
> THE FIFTY FIRE-TONGS AND FIRE-DOGS HAVE
>   FIFTY MATCHING GRATES!

MEN.
> THE SIXTY UP AND SIXTY DOWN HERE IN THE
>   STAIRCASE HALL

WOMEN.
> ARE DUSTED DAILY 'TIL YOU DON'T SEE ANY
>   DUST AT ALL

ALL *(spoken)*.
> THE WINDOWS, TABLES, CHAIRS, THE
>   SERVANTS' STAIRS,
> THE FLOOR, THE BOOTS, THE SHOES IN
>   CORNERS LURK—
> STILL LEFT TO DO!
> *(Sung.)*
> IS IT A CRIME IF WE MISS JUST A FEW!?
> *(SERVANTS exit, MEDLOCK and CRAVEN close together
> again.)*

MEDLOCK.
> MISTRESS OF MISSELTHWAITE I'M SOON TO BE

CRAVEN.
> MASTER OF ALL I SURVEY—

MEDLOCK.
> LANGUISHING LATE WHEN I'M SERVED
>   MORNING TEA

CRAVEN.
> **WELL, YOU'D BETTER GET GOING, YOU KNOW**
> **WHAT WE'RE GOING TO DO—**

BOTH.
> **IS IT A CRIME WISHFUL THINKING**
> **WITH YOU—**

(On the button, the SERVANTS' heads reappear, peeking at MEDLOCK and CRAVEN, then disappear before they notice.)

(MUSIC #6A: "WISHFUL THINKING"—
Playoff/Scene Change)

SCENE FIVE

SETTING: *Outside, the corners of several walled gardens are seen at L and R, with a central garden walk down the center, leading to a gazebo at DLC. The gazebo and the walls have low areas into which it is convenient to place a PUPPET ANIMAL from behind.*

MARY enters U, alone, looking around her new surroundings matter-of-factly, and without enthusiasm. She walks D into the gardens, and stops when she sees BEN entering midstage R.

MARY *(a bit demanding)*. What are these walls?
BEN *(hardly a glance—takes his time)*. The kitchen gardens.
MARY. Can I go in them?

BEN. If tha' likes. But there's nowt t' see. *(BEN moves U, and off. MARY walks D a bit, looking, judging. A ROBIN redbreast appears on the DR wall [a puppet, operated from behind the wall] and bursts into song.)*

MARY. Hello—a bird. *(The ROBIN sings, as if to repeat her words.)* What kind of bird are you? *(The ROBIN sings/talks again, then flies across the stage [one puppet disappears, MARY looks to the sky, second puppet appears on the other wall. MARY runs to the other wall, searches for a way in—finds no door.] To the ROBIN.)* There's no door— how do I—*(The ROBIN sings—MARY stops, realizes.)* That must be it! The Secret Garden—

(BEN reappears, U, and she runs to him.)

MARY. There's no door! This garden has no door!

BEN. What garden?

MARY. The one on the other side of this wall! There are trees there—see the tops of them—? A bird with a red breast was on the wall, and then flew off and onto one of the trees.

BEN *(whistles)*. Whew-tweet! Whew trill-tweet! *(The ROBIN returns, and they both "see" it fly over, and then onto a nearby wall.)* Here he is! *(To the ROBIN.)* Where has tha' been, tha' cheekly little beggar?

MARY. Does he always come when you call him?

BEN. Aye, that he does. When first he flew over the wall he was too weak to fly back, and we got friendly. When he went back over, the rest of the brood was gone and he was lonely, and he come back t' me.

MARY. Where did the rest of the brood fly to?

BEN. There's no knowin'. The old ones turn 'em out o' their nest and make' em fly, and they just scatter. This one was a knowin' one, and he knew he was lonely.

MARY *(stepping toward the ROBIN)*. I'm lonely.

BEN. Art tha' the little wench from India? *(She nods.)* Then no wonder tha'rt lonely.

MARY. What is your name?

BEN. Ben Weatherstaff. I'm lonely myself except when he's wi' me. He's the only friend I've got.

MARY. I have no friends at all. I never had. My ayah didn't like me and I never played with anyone.

BEN. Tha' and me was wove out o' the same cloth. We're both of us sour as we look. An' if I didn't have me work, I'd be more sour still! Sometimes work is the best play— specially when the work is makin' things sprout up from the earth, and grow and blossom. Here, lend a hand, won't you? *(Hands her a garden tool, to help him, then sings.)*

(MUSIC #7: "JUST LIKE ME")

BEN *(spoken)*.
>IF YOU FURROW YOUR FOREHEAD AND
>   SQUINT THROUGH YOUR EYES
>UNTIL YOU'RE NOT ABLE TO SEE
(Sung.)
>IF YOU PULL ON YOUR NOSE, 'TIL IT'S LONG
>   AS A HOSE,
>THEN THE CHANCES ARE QUITE GOOD, THE
>   CHANCES ARE YOU COULD
>THE CHANCES ARE YOU WOULD LOOK JUST
>   LIKE ME.

BEN *(continues, spoken).*

> BE AS GRUFF AS A BADGER, STUBBORN AS A
> STOAT,

(Sung.)

> MEAN AS A BEAR WITH A BEE
> IF YOU KEEP TO YOURSELF, TAKE NO HEED
> OF NONE ELSE
> THEN THE CHANCES ARE QUITE GOOD, THE
> CHANCES ARE YOU COULD
> THE CHANCES ARE YOU WOULD BE JUST LIKE
> ME.

> IF YOU LEARN HOW TO SPEAK WITH A SMILE
> ON YOUR CHEEK,
> BE PLEASANT TO PEOPLE YOU SEE—
> LAUGH, REALLY LAUGH, MAYBE ONCE EV'RY
> DAY,
> THEN I'D SAY THAT YOU WON'T BE LIKE ME.

***Begin cut here for one-act edition.

(Spoken.)

> IF I SCREAMED LIKE A BANSHEE, SCREECHED
> LIKE AN OWL

(Sung.)

> HOWLED LIKE A CAT UP A TREE.
> IF I SNARLED AT THE WORLD WITH MY LIPS
> TIGHTLY CURLED,
> THEN THE CHANCES ARE QUITE GOOD, THE
> CHANCES ARE I COULD,
> THE CHANCES ARE I WOULD SOUND, JUST
> LIKE THEE.

> YOU ARE YOUNG, VERY YOUNG, WHY YOU'RE
>   STILL JUST A GIRL
> YOU DON'T KNOW WHAT LIVIN' IS FOR
> AS FOR ME, I'M ACCUSTOMED TO LIFE AS IT IS—
> THE GARDEN, A ROBIN, NO MORE
> YOU CAN TAKE MY ADVICE, YOU CAN LEAVE
>   IT ALONE
> YOU'VE A CHOICE—A RARE THING TO SEE.
> YOUR SKIES CAN BE GRAY, OR BLUE EVERY DAY
> YOUR LIFE SHOULD BE ALL IT CAN BE

***Continue here for one-act edition.

BEN *(continues, spoken)*.

> I'M A MAN ON ME OWN AND I LIVE ALL ALONE
> *(Sung.)*
> IT'S THE ROAD I'VE CHOSEN FOR ME
> IF YOU DON'T CHANGE YOUR WAYS, FOR THE
>   REST OF YOUR DAYS
> THE CHANCES ARE QUITE GOOD, THE
>   CHANCES ARE YOU COULD,
> THE CHANCES ARE YOU WILL BE—JUST
>   LIKE—ME!

(After the song, the ROBIN reappears on the wall, or perhaps on the ground near MARY, who doesn't notice him.)

BEN. Well, he's made up his mind to be friends with thee.

MARY. To me? *(BEN nods; MARY turns to the ROBIN.)* Would you like to be friends with me? Would you? *(The ROBIN chirrups.)*

BEN. Why, tha' said that as nice and human as if tha' was a real child instead of a sharp ol' woman. Tha' said it almost like Dickon talks to his wild things on the moor.

MARY *(turning to BEN)*. Do you know Dickon?

BEN. Everybody knows him. Dickon's everywhere. I warrant the foxes and the skylarks know him! *(The ROBIN takes off, and flies over the wall, with a chirrup.)*

MARY. He has flown over the wall—into the garden that has no door! There must be a door somewhere.

BEN. There was ten year ago, but there isn't now.

MARY *(searching)*. There MUST be!

BEN. None as is anyone's business. Don't poke your nose where it's no cause to go. Here, I must on with my work. Get you gone and play you. I've no more time. *(Exits.)*

MARY. But—*(He is gone. She stands a moment, then runs to the wall, tries to climb it, calls over, tries to whistle like BEN did. Gives up, walks back D, sits.)*

(MUSIC #8: "WINGS")

MARY.

    IF ONLY I HAD WINGS,
    MAGIC WINGS TO GLIDE THE MOONBEAMS
    I'D FLY HOME
    HOME AGAIN

    ON WINGS, MAGIC WINGS TO RIDE THE
      RAINBOWS
    I'D FLY HOME
    HOME AGAIN—

(MARTHA enters U as if searching for MARY; sees her and approaches, and overhears the song.)

    NIGHT AFTER NIGHT I'VE BEEN DREAMING
    DREAMS,

LOVELY DREAMS OF THOSE SUNNY DAYS
I LEFT BEHIND,
ON MY WINGS, MAGIC WINGS, GLIDING
    MOONBEAMS,
I'LL FLY HOME
ON MY OWN MAGIC WINGS—

MARTHA.   MARY.

IT'S EASY TO FLY,
JUST CALL ON AN OLD
MAGIC SPELL
BELIEVING IS HOW YOU
CAN
TELL WHEN YOU'RE IN IT,
IT JUST TAKES A MINUTE
ON WINGS, GLIDING   MAGIC WINGS!
MOONBEAMS,
FLYING HOME, HOME   I'LL BE FLYING HOME
AGAIN   AGAIN *(Etc.)*

NIGHT AFTER NIGHT
I'VE BEEN DREAMING
DREAMS
LOVELY DREAMS OF
THOSE SUNNY DAYS
I LEFT BEHIND—

ON YOUR WINGS, RIDING   ON MY WINGS, RIDING
RAINBOWS   RAINBOWS,
YOU'LL BE HOME ON   HOME ON MY OWN
YOUR OWN
MAGIC WINGS   MAGIC WINGS

(On the musical tag, MARTHA slowly reaches for MARY's hand. MARY takes it on the final chord. On applause, as the set changes to the interior of the Manor, we see MEDLOCK appear to commandeer MARY, and take her inside. MARY imitates MEDLOCK's walk as she stalks off, to MARTHA's amusement, but then MEDLOCK seizes MARY and they exit.)

(MUSIC #8A "WINGS"—Playoff)

(In the transition, MARY again encounters the PORTRAIT CHILDREN. We hear MEDLOCK call "Mary Lennox!" and then see her enter. MARY takes a frame and "hides" as one of the children, then tries to slip away when MEDLOCK's back is turned, but MEDLOCK catches her, takes her off, and then down stairs into the Main Hall when the shift is ready.)

SCENE SIX

SETTING: *The Great Hall/Parlor.*

MEDLOCK and MARY are coming from Mary's room. DOCTOR CRAVEN and ARCHIE are in the UR area as the women enter DL. MARTHA trails furtively.

MEDLOCK *(out of patience).* Hush, now! You WILL have tea with your guardian, and you WILL be examined immediately afterwards by Doctor Craven—

MARY. But I heard it again, I tell you—someone is crying upstairs—

MEDLOCK. Nonsense. It must have been the wind. Or a curlew on the moor. *(A violent whisper.)* NOW MOVE!

(MEDLOCK the harridan transforms into treacle: To AR-CHIE.) Doctor Craven is here to examine Miss Mary, sir.

ARCHIE *(preoccupied)*. Ah, yes.

CRAVEN. Those were my instructions, Archie, so here I am.

MEDLOCK. I will bring Miss Mary to you after she meets with her guardian.

ARCHIE *(as MEDLOCK delays)*. Thank you, Mrs. Medlock. Richard. *(They are gone. MARY turns to look at ARCHIE, who is startled by her face momentarily.)* I trust Mrs. Medlock and Martha are looking after you properly.

MARY. Martha is looking after me properly.

ARCHIE. I see. When the weather improves you must go out for walks. There's much to see.

MARY. I know. I have already begun to explore the gardens.

ARCHIE. The gardens?

MARY. Except the one that's kept locked up.

ARCHIE. Who told you about that?

MARY. Martha did. I went out because Mrs. Medlock said I couldn't walk about inside the house. I'm to stay in my own rooms. Why is that?

ARCHIE *(harder, uneasy)*. Mrs. Medlock's orders are not to be questioned.

MARY *(abrupt, shrill)*. She treats me like a prisoner and I hate her!

ARCHIE. You will do as Mrs. Medlock says. She is in—

MARY. What's in this house that I'm not allowed to see? Who is it that cries out, day and night, down a long corridor? It's not the wind, or a bird on the moor, as Mrs. Medlock told me—or one of the maids with a toothache, as Martha says—what is it!? Please—tell me—Is it a ghost? Is this house haunted? Is the garden haunted?

ARCHIE *(leaping up, shouting)*. No! It's not haunted! There are no ghosts here! *(Pause. Calmer.)* Leave me now.

Please. *(MUSIC.)* Go away from me. PLEASE. Go up-stairs…back to your rooms.

MARY *(almost in tears).* Why? What have I done?

ARCHIE. Go AWAY FROM ME! *(He turns from her. He is haunted.)* I can't…look at you…I see only the face of someone I hoped you might…No. It's no good. Just go away from me, Mary, please—

(MUSIC #9: "SOMEWHERE IN THE PAST")

(MARY hides on the stair. ARCHIE turns to look at the portrait of Lilian, then sings. During the song, MARY listens and watches. The "Lily" portrait on the wall comes alive.)

ARCHIE.
>   SOMEWHERE IN THE PAST
>   EVERY DAY WAS NEW
>   MORNING AIR WAS SWEETER THEN
>   SKIES A BRIGHTER BLUE

(LILIAN moves out of the frame, and down the stairs to ARCHIE.)

>   I REMEMBER SMILES
>   LAUGHING EYES OF BLUE
>   SOMEONE'S HAND ENCLOSED IN MINE,
>   PRECIOUS TIME SPENT WITH SOMEONE
>   WHO COULD CHANGE A STORMY DAY FROM
>   DARK
>   TO SHINING GREY
>   AND SILVER RAIN BECAME THE SOFTEST
>   KISS—HOW I MISS

(LILIAN dances around ARCHIE, who is surrounded by memories of her.)

> SOMEONE IN MY ARMS
> SOMEONE'S GENTLE TOUCH
> I COULD NEVER LOVE AS MUCH,
> CARE AS MUCH, LIVE AGAIN
> FOR SOMEONE NEW—
> WHEN SOMEWHERE IN THE PAST,
> THERE WAS YOU...
>
> *(An instrumental break, PORTRAIT PEOPLE emerge from their frames, and dance.)*

PORTRAIT ENSEMBLE.
> SOMEWHERE IN THE PAST I WAS JUST LIKE YOU
> ONCE UPON A WAY BACK WHEN I WAS
> LONELY FOR SOMEONE—

ARCHIE & LILIAN *(ENSEMBLE in support).*
> WHO COULD CHANGE A STORMY DAY FROM
> DARK TO SHINING GREY
> AND SILVER RAIN BECAME THE SOFTEST
> KISS—HOW I MISS

ARCHIE.
> SOMEONE IN MY ARMS, SOMEONE'S GENTLE
> TOUCH

ARCHIE *(with ENSEMBLE aaahs).*
> I COULD NEVER LOVE AS MUCH
> CARE AS MUCH, LIVE AGAIN FOR SOMEONE
> NEW—

ARCHIE.
> WHEN SOMEWHERE IN THE PAST
> THERE WAS YOU.

(As the song ends, and the final "you" is held, LILIAN returns behind her gauze of memory, and the PORTRAIT PEOPLE return to their frames, sadly. ARCHIE finds himself again looking at MARY's face, for the girl has moved near him. He breaks away, and exits.)

(MUSIC #9A: "SOMEWHERE IN THE PAST"—Playoff)

(A tapestry flies in D to suggest a hallway. In the hallway, a line of PORTRAIT CHILDREN appear in the transition.)

MARY *(to the CHILDREN)*. Listen! *(They do.)* It's nearer than it was—and it IS crying! Come on!

(The CHILDREN join MARY in a tiptoe search excursion. MUSIC under. MEDLOCK appears instantly, terrifying all.)

MEDLOCK. WHAT ARE YOU DOING HERE! *(The POR-TRAIT CHILDREN scramble rapidly, and a bit crookedly assume their portrait positions.)*

MARY. I turned the wrong way. I didn't know which way to go, and I heard SOMEONE CRYING!

MEDLOCK. You didn't hear anything of the sort. You come along back to your own nursery or I'll box your ears!

(MUSIC #9B: "WISHFUL THINKING"—Scene change)

(MEDLOCK drags MARY off and the setting for Mary's room appears, complete with MARTHA. MARY and MEDLOCK re-enter.)

MEDLOCK. You stay where you're told to or you'll find yourself locked up! I think the master had best get you a governess! *(This a jab at MARTHA.)* You're one that needs someone to look sharp after you. I've enough to do! *(She stalks off.)*

SCENE SEVEN

SETTING: *Mary's room.*

MARY shrugs off MARTHA's effort to comfort her.

MARY. There WAS someone crying. There Was! *(MARTHA turns to her as if to speak—but then stops, turns away, shaking her head.)* I can't walk about the house because of Mrs. Medlock. I can't go outside and find the robin because it's raining again.

MARTHA. The robin?

MARY. The robin who lives in the Secret Garden. Ben Weatherstaff's friend. And he might be my friend, too, but not if I never go see him. And Ben was starting to show me how to plant things, and make them grow. But he can't if it's windy and cold and keeps RAINING every day so I can't even go outside *(She dissolves in tears.)*

MARTHA *(helping her into her nightgown)*. Eh! You mustn't cry like that! You mustn't for sure. Don't be vexed by Mrs. Medlock. She's just a dark cloud that'll blow over. *(Pause.)* And if you and Ben are plantin' things, the rain'll be good for them!

MARY *(still upset)*. But all it DOES is rain, or look dark. That's all it does in England.

MARTHA *(embracing and tucking MARY into bed)*. Aah, no, Miss Mary, the springtime's comin'! What if I have Dickon bring you some of his seeds to plant with Ben?!

Some flower seeds to bloom in the summer sunshine. *(MARY nods just a little.)* Oh, the summer! It's a long way off yet, but the summer sunshine is comin' to make your flowers bloom! *(MARTHA settles MARY down and dims the lamp.)*

(MUSIC #10: "BEFORE YOU KNOW, IT'S SUMMER")

MARTHA *(sings).*
>THE EVENING WIND IS BOLD
>THE MORNING DARK AND GREY.
>THE AIR IS BITTER COLD,
>THE SUN JUST HIDES AWAY.
(MARY sleeps, MARTHA steps D into isolated light.)
>BUT WHILE A DREARY WORLD IS SLEEPING
>THROUGH THE WINTER TIME,
>THE CLOCK TICKS ON
>IT WON'T BE LONG.

(The next morning. MARY wakes to a brilliant sun streaming in her window, and eagerly dresses herself to go out. MARTHA steps back into the scene with Mary's porridge, which she eats eagerly. Then runs to the window and prepares to go out.)

>THERE WILL BE A SKY
>BLUE AS BLUE AGAIN,
>SILVER MORNING DEW AGAIN.
>IT SPARKLES AND GLISTENS,
>LISTEN AND YOU'LL HEAR
>THE BIRDS ARE HUMMING 'ROUND,
>BEES ARE BUZZING 'ROUND
>TOUCH A YELLOW BUTTERFLY

> AS IT FLUTTERS BY,
> WATCH A BABY BIRD TRY—

(MARTHA reminds MARY to straighten up her bed, tosses the pillow to her in fun.)

> THERE WILL BE A DAY
> CLEAR AND BRIGHT AGAIN
> WHEN CLOUDS ARE PILLOW-WHITE AGAIN
> DANDELIONS FLY,
> CATCH A FALLING STAR,

(MARY starts out, MARTHA points to her coat, then helps her button it up. MARY is ready.)

> RIDE THE RAINBOW FAR AS YOU CAN SEE,
> BEFORE YOU KNOW IT'S SUMMER
> AND ALL THAT SUMMER WILL BE.

(MARTHA nods, moves D, MARY bursts running from the room, as the room itself bursts open in a scene shift that returns us to the gardens with MARY, and with MARTHA watching. ARCHIE, back from a solitary walk, also sees the running child.)

MARTHA *(continues).*

> THERE WILL BE A DAY
> CLEAR AND BRIGHT AGAIN
> WHEN CLOUDS ARE PILLOW-WHITE AGAIN,
> DANDELIONS FLY,

(The ROBIN appears high in the sky as MARY runs D past the gazebo, waving to him. She turns, waves to MARTHA, who waves back. And then, surprisingly, MARY notices ARCHIE, and waves. He pauses a moment, then shyly raises a hand and almost waves back.)

> CATCH A FALLING STAR ,
> RIDE THE RAINBOW FAR AS YOU CAN SEE

BEFORE YOU KNOW IT'S SUMMER
AND ALL THAT SUMMER
WILL BE

SCENE EIGHT

SETTING: *Outside among the gardens, as in Scene Five.*

MARY turns from MARTHA and runs about the gardens with exuberance, sees BEN coming from U and runs to walk down with him.

MARY. BEN! BEN!

BEN. Springtime's comin'—you'll see bits o' green spikes stickin' out o' the black earth after a bit *(He gestures to a spot, and MARY rushes to get down on the ground and look. The ROBIN appears and sings, on the ground if possible, or on the gazebo wall.)*

MARY. Look, Ben! Do you think he remembers me?

BEN. Remembers thee? He's bent on findin' all about thee! Tha's no need to try to hide anythin' from HIM.

MARY. Are green spikes stickin' up and leaves uncurling in that garden where he lives, too?

BEN. What garden?

MARY. The one he always flies to—without the door!

BEN *(exiting)*. Ask him. He's the only one as knows. No one else has been inside it for ten year. *(MARY walks over near the wall of the robin's garden, and the ROBIN flies near her, perhaps onto the wall, or the ground nearby.)*

MARY. You DO remember me! You do! You are prettier than anything else in the world! *(She chirps and "talks"*

*with him, drawing close to the ROBIN, who is on the
ground now, near the wall. The ROBIN is busy scratching,
trying to pull things from the earth.)* Chirrup, chirrup! What
are you scratching for, Mr. Robin? Is it worms? *(The ROBIN
stops a moment, then pecks twice and moves away.)* Let me
see—why, you've found something—*(She picks it up.)*—

(MUSIC #10A: "PERCUSSION—SOUND CUES")

MARY *(continues)*. it's a KEY! Buried in the ground! *(She
stops—whispers to the ROBIN.)* Perhaps it has been buried
for TEN YEARS! *(The ROBIN chirps.)* Perhaps it is the
KEY TO THE GARDEN! *(The ROBIN chirps brightly,
"flies" up onto a high perch in his garden. MARY follows
the ROBIN to the wall, where she notices something under
the ivy.)* What—there's something here—*(She brushes aside
some ivy.)*—Why, It's a DOOR! *(She tries the key in the
lock, and the door opens.)* Oh, Thank you, robin—THANK
YOU!

(MUSIC #11: "DICKON IS MY NAME")

*(She steps just inside the doorway, and then is stopped by
the sound of a flute or recorder. She looks for the source of
the sound, and then looks back at the Secret Garden, lean-
ing toward it, anxious to enter—but then she sees a teen-
age BOY approaching, and closes the door to protect her
secret. The BOY comes D to the gazebo, where he whistles up
puppet characters with his flute, a FOX and a CROW, and
perhaps a SQUIRREL or two. MARY steps forward to him.)*

DICKON. Don't tha' move—it'd flight 'em. *(He plays for a
moment more, MUSIC: "DICKON'S SONG," then very*

slowly gets up, and the ANIMALS withdraw.) I know thee—Tha's Miss Mary.

MARY. And you're Dickon! You talk to the animals and birds! Martha says you understand everything they say.

DICKON. I think I do—and they think I do! *(During the song, the ANIMALS may reappear and listen, including the ROBIN.)*
> I CAN MAKE A HEDGEHOG WHISTLE—
> ANYTHING YOU ASK.
> I CAN PICK A PRICKLY THISTLE,
> THAT'S AN EASY TASK,
> THE BLUEBIRD ON THE RAINBOW,
> THE ROBIN ON THE WING
> CALL ME DICKON
> KNOW I'M DICKON
> CALL ME DICKON—
> DICKON IS MY NAME

***Begin cut here for one-act edition

> I CAN HEAR THE FOXES RUNNING
> FAR ACROSS THE MOOR
> I CAN SEE A SPIDER SPINNING
> THROUGH HIS TINY DOOR
> ASK ME HOW THE WILD GOOSE
> KNOWS IT'S TIME TO GO—
> 'CAUSE I'VE LIVED EACH DAY THE SAME,
> WITH THE CREATURES WHO KNOW—
> DICKON IS MY...

> NAME ME A RIVER,
> FIND ME A FOREST,
> FIND ME A FIELD I DON'T KNOW
> SHOW ME THE HEATHER WHEN

MORNING FIRST SEES IT
I'LL SAY I GOT THERE
BEFORE IT WARMED IT.

***Continue here for one-act edition

I CAN SHOW YOU PATHS TO FOLLOW, RUN
AND LAUGH LIKE ME
SEE THAT CLEVER LITTLE SWALLOW, HE
LEARNED TO FLY LIKE ME

YOU CAN FLY TOMORROW, YOU WILL WALK
TODAY—
FOLLOW DICKON, WALK WITH DICKON.
FLY WITH DICKON, I WILL SHOW THE WAY!
(Spoken.) See here, Miss Mary, the seeds Martha asked me
to bring to you.

MARY. Ohhhh—thank you! *(Takes the seeds.)* I shall plant
them, and they'll grow forever! FOREVER!

(BEN has entered.)

MARY. Ben! Ben Weatherstaff!
BEN. Well, now, here's Dickon! And Miss Mary—what are
you so full of?
MARY. Dickon has brought me some seeds to plant—Ben, if
you had a garden of your own, what would you plant?
BEN. Oh, cabbages, and onions, and 'taters—
MARY. But if you wanted a FLOWER garden, what would
you plant?
BEN. Bulbs an' sweet smellin' things—but mostly roses.
MARY. Do you like roses?

BEN. Yes, I do—

MARY. When they have no leaves, and are grey and brown and dry—how can you tell if they are dead or alive?

BEN. Why does tha' care so much about roses and such, all of a sudden?

MARY. I—I want to play that—well, Dickon has brought me these seeds, and I want to play that I have a garden of my own—

BEN. Well, then, get thee gone and play thee. Dickon can help thee. I've done talkin' today. *(He exits.)*

DICKON. Where's tha' garden? I'll plant the seeds for ye meself. *(MARY stops, turns aside.)* Tha's got a bit o' garden, hasn't tha'? *(MARY doesn't answer.)* Haven't they given thee a bit?

MARY. Could you keep a secret, if I told you one? It's a great secret. If anyone found it out, I think I should die!

DICKON. I'm keepin' secrets all the time. If I couldn't keep secrets from the other lads—secrets about fox's cubs, and birds' nests, the wild things'd not be safe on the moor. Aye, I can keep secrets.

MARY. I've stolen a garden! It isn't mine, but nobody wants it, nobody cares for it, nobody ever goes into it.

DICKON. Where is it?

MARY. Come with me, and I'll show you. *(She leads him to the ivy-covered wall, and lifts up the ivy that covers the door.)* It's here! *(She opens the door.)* It's a Secret Garden, and I'm the only one in the world that wants it to be alive!

(MUSIC #11B: "BEFORE YOU KNOW, IT'S SUMMER"
—Transition)

(Bird whistles, crow caws, animal antics. Lights transition to dark, quickly, as we hear thunder and moaning and wailing.)

SCENE NINE

SETTING: *In the Manor, the Hall/Parlor.*

ARCHIE appears in a special, beginning his song as the scenery finishes changing around him. MARTHA is with MARY, who whispers to her.

(MUSIC #12: "I'VE GOT A SECRET")

ARCHIE.
　　YOU SEE THIS LITTLE GIRL WHO'S COME TO STAY
　　SHE RUSHES IN WITH SO MANY THINGS TO SAY
(MARY rushes forward like a freight train, then catches herself charmingly, and curtsies to ARCHIE, ladylike but desperately eager to speak with him. She sits.)
　　AS IF HER DAY WERE FULL OF THOSE
　　　MAGICAL PROMISES
　　SOMEONE ONCE PROMISED FOR ME

　　AND NOW IN THIS PAIR OF EYES THERE'S NO
　　　DISGUISE, COULD SHE
(Spoken.) I wonder—
　　SHE NEED ME—
(ARCHIE, MARTHA and MEDLOCK freeze as MARY sings, in an aside, to the audience and the PORTRAIT CHILDREN, sharing her excitement with PORTRAIT PEOPLE and CHILDREN.)

MARY.
>I'VE GOT A SECRET, A SECRET, A SECRET,
>DEEP AS A WELL—
>I'VE GOT A SECRET, A SECRET, A SECRET,
>I'LL NEVER TELL!
>DID YOU KNOW THE STARS KEEP THE SUNLIGHT,
>THE SUNLIGHT RIGHT NEXT TO THEIR BED?
>EACH MORNING A STAR PACKS HIS KNAPSACK
>WITH SUNLIGHT AND TRAVELS ALL DAY
>'TIL HE FINDS A PLACE TO STAY,
>OPENS HIS KNAPSACK AND TAKES OUT THE
>   LIGHT
>IN CASE HE SHOULD WAKE IN THE NIGHT AND
>   BE SCARED.
>A STAR KEEPS THE SUNLIGHT NEXT TO HIS BED.

PORTRAIT PEOPLE.
>I'VE GOT A SECRET, A SECRET, A SECRET
>DEEP AS A WELL
>I'VE GOT A SECRET, A SECRET, A SECRET,
>I'll NEVER TELL
>*(MARY returns to the chair as the ADULTS unfreeze.)*

ARCHIE.
>SUDDENLY THIS LITTLE GIRL SEEMS TO PULL
>   ALL THE STRINGS OF MY HEART
>*(PORTRAIT PEOPLE are moved.)*
>SUDDENLY ALL I CAN SEE IS A FACE THAT
>   REMINDS ME OF ROSES

MEDLOCK.
>THIS GIRL NEEDS A GOVERNESS, THEN SHE
>   WOULD MIND

ARCHIE.
IN SUMMER

MARTHA.
AND SHE NEEDS OTHER CHILDREN AND
SOMEONE WHO'S KIND

ARCHIE.
LILACS

MARY.
MOST WONDERFUL THINGS, DO YOU THINK
THEY SUSPECT?

ARCHIE.
IN SPRING

MARY.
WHO ELSE CAN I ASK, WHO'D BE KNOWING
SO MUCH
(ADULTS freeze.)
DID YOU KNOW THE SKY WEARS A
TAILOR-MADE COAT
WHEN IT'S RAINY AND GREY.
JUST ANY OLD COAT WOULDN'T FIT
IF IT'S BITTER AND WINDY ALL DAY.

SO SKY BUYS AN EXTRA LARGE BLANKET OF
CLOUD FOR HIS TAILOR TO SEW
AND THAT'S HOW I KNOW SKY IS COZY AND DRY.
WRAPPED IN THE BEST COAT THAT MONEY
CAN BUY

MARY, PORTRAIT PEOPLE, PORTRAIT CHILDREN.
> I'VE GOT A SECRET, A SECRET, A SECRET,
> DEEP AS A WELL; I'VE GOT A SECRET, A
> SECRET, A SECRET,
> I'LL NEVER TELL.
> *(MARY finishes back in the chair, portraits back on "wall"*
> *as ADULTS unfreeze.)*
> I'VE GOT A SECRET, A SECRET, A SECRET,
> DEEP AS A WELL,
> I'VE GOT A SECRET, A SECRET, A SECRET
> I'LL NEVER TELL!

ARCHIE. —so, it was thoughtless of me to say…the things I said to you when you first arrived. I was not myself, and you must forgive me. *(Pause.)*

MARY. Oh, of course I do, sir. *(She smiles, a strategy to get what she wants.)*

ARCHIE. Now, while you're here—what would you like to do—?

MARY. Well, sir—might I be permitted to keep playing out of doors? *(Pause, glancing at him.)* It makes me feel strong when I play, and the wind comes over the moor…

ARCHIE. Where do you play?

MARY. Everywhere! I skip, and run—I look to see if things are beginning to stick up out of the earth…I don't do any harm—

ARCHIE. Don't look so frightened, child—you couldn't do any harm—*(MEDLOCK starts to speak.)*—you may do what you like.

MARY. May I!?

ARCHIE. Of course you may. Is there anything you want— toys, dolls, books?

MARY. Might I—might I have a bit of earth?

ARCHIE. Earth? What do you mean?

MARY. To plant seeds in—to make things grow—to see them come alive.

ARCHIE *(after a pause—distant, in memory)*. A bit of earth...*(He looks at her, moved.)* You can have as much earth as you want. You remind me of...someone else, who loved the earth, and things that grow. *(He smiles at her, for the first time.)* Take it, child, and make it come alive.

MARY. May I take it from anywhere, if it's not wanted?

ARCHIE. Anywhere. *(Pause, as they look at each other. He breaks it.)* There! *(Covering his emotions.)* You must go now, I am very tired. Good-bye. I shall be away all summer. *(MUSIC under: "I'VE GOT A SECRET" slow lead-in to tag/reprise.)*

MARY. Good-bye, sir. *(She curtsies.)* And thank you. *(She smiles, this time genuinely. MUSIC up, Transition: "I'VE GOT A SECRET." ARCHIE exits. MARY dashes from MEDLOCK and off.)*

(MUSIC #12A: "I'VE GOT A SECRET"—Playoff)

ENSEMBLE *(as the transition is made)*.
   I'VE GOT A SECRET A SECRET, A SECRET,
   DEEP AS A WELL

(MEDLOCK is joined by CRAVEN in a dark corner of the scene shift. He kisses her hand as they sing with the EN-SEMBLE.)

MEDLOCK, CRAVEN, ENSEMBLE.
   I'VE GOT A SECRET, A SECRET, A SECRET,
   I'LL NEVER TELL—!

***The optional song and dialogue intro at end of script (page 103) may be inserted here if the director wishes to include the song "TRADITIONS," which may be performed as a duet for CRAVEN and MEDLOCK. The authors, however, have chosen to cut it. If SCENE NINE-B is inserted here, then MUSIC #12B "TRADITIONS" and MUSIC #12C: "TRANSITIONS/SCENE CHANGE" are here.)

(CRAVEN chases MEDLOCK off, and they depart with a whoop and a giggle. The mood shifts as we hear thunder and crying, and the PORTRAIT CHILDREN enter to form their hallway line, and are joined by MARY.)

SCENE TEN

SETTING: *Dark hallways, then Colin's room. Wind and rain.*

MARY *(to PORTRAIT CHILDREN)*. That ISN'T the wind. That's the crying I heard before *(The crying again.)* I am going to find out what it is. Everybody is in bed, and I don't care about Mrs. Medlock. I don't care!

(More thunder, darkness, and MARY and the CHILDREN emerge into Colin's room. As his bed is rolled in, he lies tossing and crying. MARY walks closer.)

COLIN. Hah! *(His eyes open wide—a half whisper.)* Who are you? *(Pause.)* Are you a ghost?
MARY *(also a whisper, eyes just as wide)*. No. Are you one!
COLIN. No. *(Pause. They hold their candles up toward one another.)* I'm Colin Craven.

MARY. I am Mary Lennox. Mr. Craven is my uncle.

COLIN. He is my father. But he doesn't come to see me.

MARY. Why?

COLIN. My mother died when I was born, and it makes him wretched to look at me. He almost hates me.

MARY *(to herself)*. He hates the garden, because she died.

COLIN. What garden?

MARY. Oh, just—just a garden she used to like. *(Pause.)*

COLIN. How old are you?

MARY. I am ten. And so are you.

COLIN. How do you know that!

MARY. Because when you were born the garden was locked, and the key was buried. It has been locked for ten years, and there's no door.

COLIN. No door? It must have a door if it had a key. *(MARY shakes her head.)* Don't you want to see it?

MARY. Yes.

COLIN. I do, yes! I don't think I ever wanted to see anything before, but I want to see that garden. I would let them take me there in my chair. I am going to make them open the door.

MARY. Oh! Don't—don't—Don't do that!

COLIN. Why? You said you wanted to see it.

MARY *(almost in tears)*. I do—but if you make them open the door like that it will never have a secret again!

COLIN. A secret? What do you mean?

MARY. If—If you won't make THEM take you to the garden—perhaps—I feel almost sure that I can find out how to get in sometime, and perhaps might find some boy who would push your chair, and we could go alone, and it would always be a secret garden.

COLIN. I should like that. I should not mind fresh air in a secret garden. I think you shall be a secret, too. *(Pause.)* I am going to let you look at something. *(COLIN gestures to a portrait.*) She is my mother. I believe if she had lived, I would not have been ill always. And my father would not have hated to look at me.

(MUSIC #13: "MY MOTHER")

COLIN.
>IF MOTHER COULD BE HERE SHE'D HOLD ME
>>SO TIGHT
>
>I'D NEVER BE LONELY OR CRY IN THE NIGHT
>SHE'D SING TO ME, TALK TO ME, THEN DIM
>>THE LIGHT
>
>AND NEVER FORGET TO KISS ME GOOD NIGHT
>AND NEVER FORGET TO KISS ME GOOD NIGHT

MARY.
>MY MOTHER WAS BEAUTIFUL HAPPY AND GAY
>SHE GLIDED THROUGH LIFE IN A MAGICAL WAY

MARY & PORTRAIT CHILDREN *(in unison)*.
>SHE LAUGHED AND HER EYES SHONE EVER SO
>>BRIGHT
>
>BUT SHE NEVER CAME IN TO KISS ME GOOD NIGHT

*** possible cut

>MY MOTHER'S IN HEAVEN, SHE'S ALL
>>DRESSED IN WHITE
>
>SOMETIMES I SEE HER DEEP IN THE NIGHT
>SHE WHISPERS SHE LOVES ME, AND CALMS
>>ALL MY FEARS
>
>AND SOMETIMES HER EYES ARE ALL FILLED
>>WITH TEARS

> **AND SOMETIMES HER EYES ARE ALL FILLED
> WITH TEARS.**

*** end possible cut

MARY, COLIN & CHILDREN.
> **WHY, WHY CAN'T MOTHER BE HERE
> I'M LONELY, AND FRETFUL, AND ALWAYS IN
> TEARS
> SHE'D WHISPER SHE LOVES ME AND CALM
> ALL MY FEARS,
> I'D NEVER BE LONELY IF MOTHER WERE HERE**

COLIN *(& LILLIAN in parenthesis) (& CHILDREN, below)*.
> **IF MOTHER COULD BE HERE SHE'D HOLD
> ME(YOU) SO TIGHT
> I'D(YOU'D) NEVER BE LONELY OR CRY IN THE
> NIGHT
> SHE'D SING TO ME(YOU), TALK TO ME(YOU),
> THEN DIM THE LIGHT
> AND NEVER FORGET TO KISS ME(YOU) GOOD
> NIGHT**

LILIAN *(simultaneously with MARY below)*.
> **MOTHER IS HERE TO HOLD YOU SO TIGHT,
> YOU'LL NEVER BE LONELY OR CRY IN THE
> NIGHT
> I'LL SING TO YOU, TALK TO YOU, THEN DIM
> THE LIGHT
> AND NEVER FORGET TO KISS YOU GOOD NIGHT**

MARY *(simultaneously with LILIAN above)*.
> **MOTHER WAS BEAUTIFUL, HAPPY AND GAY,**

**SHE GLIDED THROUGH LIFE IN A WHIMSICAL
WAY
SHE LAUGHED AND HER EYES SHONE EVER SO
BRIGHT
BUT SHE NEVER CAME IN TO KISS ME GOOD
NIGHT**

MARY & COLIN.
**I WISH SHE WERE HERE TO KISS ME GOOD
NIGHT**

*(MARY tucks COLIN in as MARTHA enters on applause;
PORTRAIT CHILDREN run and hide, and may exit.)*

MARTHA. Eh! Miss Mary! Tha' shouldn't have come here! I
never told thee nothin' about Master Colin—but tha'll get
me in trouble! Mrs. Medlock will send me away—

MARY. He was glad I came! He wouldn't let me go! And he
says everybody is obliged to do as he pleases. Even Mrs.
Medlock!

MARTHA. Aye, that's true enough—the bad lad.

COLIN. Well, then, if I ORDER you to bring Miss Mary to
me, how can Medlock send you away if she finds out?

MARTHA. But, sir, I...

COLIN. I'll send HER away if she dares to bother you! So.
You will send Mary to me when I ask. Now go away.

MARTHA *(about to explode at being spoken to this way)*.
Beggin' your pardon, sir, but I'll not...

MARY *(interposing herself)*. You know, Colin—You are a
very spoiled boy. *(Folds her arms, shakes her head, and
looks down at him.)* I was thinking how different you are
from Dickon.

COLIN. Who is Dickon?

MARY. Dickon is Martha's brother. He is fourteen, and not like anyone in the world. He can charm foxes and squirrels and birds. He lives on the moor so much he knows their ways.

COLIN. The moor?

MARTHA. When Dickon talks of the moor you feel as if you are standing in the heather with the sun shining and the gorse full of bees and butterflies.

COLIN. I couldn't go on the moor! I am going to die.

MARY. How do you know?

COLIN. Oh, I've heard it ever since I can remember. Medlock and Craven are always whispering about it and thinking I don't notice. When I had typhoid, they looked like chipmunks.

MARY (*pointedly*). I don't believe that any more than I believe you can't go out in the gardens, like me—or out on the moor, like Dickon. Oh, let's do it, Martha—let's take him outside! Dickon can help us! It will be our secret—all of us!

COLIN. I'm going to die, and I'm going to do it in here.

MARTHA. Aye, 'tis true. Die ye will, in here. Here's the remains of a world of knights and ladies that's covered with dust. But out there—that's the Lord's world. (*Sings.*)

(MUSIC #14: "SOMETHING SPECIAL")

**WHEN YOU HEAR A ROBIN SING
SOMETHING SPECIAL HAPPENS WHEN A
ROBIN SINGS
AND WHEN YOU SEE LILACS BLOOM IN SPRING
ALL THE WORLD'S BEEN SLEEPING IN ITS
COZY BED
THEN SOMETHING SPECIAL HAPPENS TO
WAKE UP ITS SLEEPY HEAD**

AND LATE AT NIGHT WHEN YOU'RE ALONE,
SOMETHING SPECIAL HAPPENS SO YOU'RE
   NOT ALONE
JUST CLOSE YOUR EYES, YOUR HEART
   KNOWS WHAT TO SAY
NOW I LAY ME DOWN TO SLEEP, AND THANK
   THEE FOR THIS DAY

AND ONE THING'S CERTAIN
VERY CERTAIN
SOMETHING SPECIAL HAPPENS THAT WAY

(During an instrumental break, MARTHA and MARY draw COLIN from his bed, with great effort, into a wheelchair, and roll him D to the "window," where they draw back the "drapes," bringing brilliant sunshine into the room. At the same time the bedroom tapestry flies out, to reveal the U exterior, including the GARDENERS, SERVANTS and BEN. Side scrim sections of the manor interior may remain, in which PORTRAIT PEOPLE join the song, along with PORTRAIT CHILDREN—if they are still on. LILIAN enters.)

MARTHA, PORTRAIT PEOPLE, PORTRAIT CHILDREN.
   AND WHEN YOU HEAR A ROBIN SING,
   SOMETHING SPECIAL HAPPENS WHEN A
      ROBIN SINGS,
   AND WHEN YOU SEE LILACS BLOOM IN SPRING
   NOW I LAY ME DOWN TO SLEEP, AND THANK
      THEE FOR THIS DAY
   AND ONE THING'S CERTAIN
   VERY CERTAIN

SOMETHING SPECIAL
HAPPENS THAT WAY

(COLIN hugs MARTHA, and LILIAN has drawn close. As the final fanfare plays, LILIAN brushes his cheek with a kiss—he reacts, having felt a joy he can't explain. The lights fade out.)

END ACT ONE

ACT TWO

(MUSIC #15: "ENTRACTE")

SETTING: *At the Gazebo.*

(MUSIC #15A: "I'VE GOT A SECRET"—Reprise)

MARY & DICKON *(as FOX and CROW sway at gazebo).*
**I'VE GOT A SECRET, A SECRET, A SECRET,
DEEP AS A WELL—
I'VE GOT A SECRET, A SECRET, A SECRET, I'LL
NEVER TELL—!**

CROW & FOX *(imitating melody and MARY, DICKON).*
CAW, CA CAW CAAAAAW *(FOX with fox sounds.)*

MARY *(continuing a conversation with DICKON).* Hush now, Soot, Captain—this is important. *(CROW caws.)*
DICKON. The servants say Master Craven can't bear to see Colin because his eyes is so like his mother's, and 'cause he fears one day the boy will grow hunchback. *(CROW and FOX look at each other.)*
MARY. Colin's so afraid of that himself that he won't sit up. He says that if he should feel a lump coming he should go crazy and scream himself to death. *(CROW caws as if screaming himself to death, flops onto his back, plays dead.)*

DICKON. Yes, Soot, he'd scream just like that. Eh! If he was out here he wouldn't be watchin' for lumps to grow on his back. *(CROW caws.)* He'd be watchin' for buds to break on the rose bushes, and he'd be healthier. *(Caw! FOX swats CROW.)*

MARY. We'll do it. We'll just have to do it. To bring him to the garden without anybody knowing.

(BEN approaches.)

BEN. Well, Mistress Mary, quite contrary, how does your garden grow?
    With Dickon's aid, and a fine old spade, and tulip bulbs all in a row—

MARY. Ben Weatherstaff, stop your teasing. You know I don't like that poem.

BEN. Master Dickon—doesn't tha' find Mistress Mary here quite contrary like the rhyme?

DICKON *(grinning and playing along)*. Ah, quite, quite the most contrary lass I've seen.

MARY *(a theatrical huff)*. I'll thank you both to leave me alone. You are both horrid. Here I am trying to find a way to help a friend, and neither of you will help me.

BEN. Friend? Ah, the lass has friends, now! When I first saw her she was so contrary she couldna find a soul to talk to but the robin—and pretty soon he would fly away.

MARY *(remembering)*. That's true. And I do have friends now *(Looks at them)*. Don't I?

BEN. Well, if you'd call friends a broken-down gardener and a boy who talks to animals—Aye, lass, I'd say you do. *(Pause.)* And who's tha' third friend?

MARY *(glances at DICKON—a warning—moves away a bit, distant)*. Oh, just a—a friend. He's just so lonely—

BEN. Hmm. I see. Could it be Master Archibald tha'
means—? *(MARY shakes her head, DICKON signals not to
press her.)* Well, no matter—just tell your friend to put his
best foot forward—and you do the same.

MARY. What do you mean?

(MUSIC #16: "YOUR BEST FOOT")

BEN. It's like anything in life. Don't SIT there broodin'—get
up and get along! *(Sings.)*
**WHEN YOU'RE LONELY
REMEMBER THERE'S ONLY
ONE THING THAT YOU HAVE TO DO**

**JUST PUT YOUR LEFT FOOT
THEN YOUR BEST FOOT
FORWARD IN FRONT OF YOU**

**SO IF IT'S RAINING
THERE'S NO NEED COMPLAINING
THE SENSIBLE THING TO DO**

**IS PUT YOUR LEFT FOOT
THEN YOUR BEST FOOT
FORWARD IN FRONT OF YOU**

**IF WHAT YOU'VE GOT
IS NOT A LOT
IT'S WHAT YOU DO, NOT WHAT YOU GET
THAT MAKES YOU STRONG AND DON'T
    FORGET
THIS WORLD WON'T TURN FOR YOU!**

SO KEEP YOUR CHIN UP
AND EVEN A GRIN UP YOUR SLEEVE
WILL SHOW THEM WHO'S WHO
AND ONE LITTLE LEFT FOOT
WILL LEAD TO THE NEXT FOOT
THE REST IS UP TO YOU
WITH ONE LITTLE LEFT FOOT
YOU'LL LEAD TO YOUR BEST FOOT
AND THAT'S THE BEST YOU CAN DO

(Instrumental, dance of teasing and horseplay and "one foot" then the other, turns into a soft shoe among BEN, MARY and DICKON.)

IT'S WHAT YOU DO NOT WHAT YOU GET
THAT MAKES YOU STRONG, AND DON'T
   FORGET
THIS WORLD WON'T STOP FOR YOU

ALL.

SO KEEP YOUR CHIN UP
AND EVEN A GRIN UP YOUR SLEEVE
WILL SHOW THEM WHO'S WHO

BEN.

AND ONE LITTLE LEFT FOOT

MARY & DICKON.

WILL LEAD TO THE NEXT FOOT

ALL.

THE REST IS UP TO YOU

BEN.

WITH ONE LITTLE LEFT FOOT

MARY & DICKON.
>YOU'LL BE ON YOUR BEST FOOT

ALL.
>AND THAT'S THE BEST—
>YOU CAN DOOOOOO—*(Lights darken.)*

>(MUSIC #16A: "YOUR BEST FOOT"—
>Playoff/Transition)

SCENE TWO

SETTING: *Colin's room.*

COLIN *(in a tantrum, at MARTHA).* TODAY! TODAAAA-AY! *(He throws things off the bed, including the pillow, which MARTHA retrieves.)*

MARTHA. PLEASE, Master Colin, Please!—She's not even supposed to know you are HERE—how can I—

COLIN. I DON'T WANT TO BE HERE! I WANT TO DIE!

(MEDLOCK and other SERVANTS rush in, including the NURSE, who brings a sedative [injection? pills? ether in a cloth?—1911?.)

COLIN. I WANT TO DIE AND FLY FAR FROM HERE—FAR AWAY! AWAY!—

MEDLOCK *(soothing him as he struggles).* That's the boy, now. That's my good boy. Sweet and quiet now, sweet as an angel—that's right—sweet as an angel—just like an angel. Be an angel. Sweet and quiet like an angel. Like an angel...(*He has exhausted himself, and the medicine begins to take effect. The SERVANTS, led by MEDLOCK, buzz about, calm him, shush one another and leave. MARTHA delays, shakes her head.*)

MARTHA. Good day, Master Colin. I'm sorry you're un-happy, sir—but as long as we're sharin' secrets—my secret thought is you've got no reason to throw such a tantrum. (*He turns away.*) Miss Mary will be back soon, I'm sure. (*She sighs and leaves, he sits up as if to speak, but she is gone, and he regrets being left alone. He sighs and looks about him, throws an object weakly.*)

(MUSIC #17: "I DON'T WANT TO BE AN ANGEL")

COLIN.
> PLEASE GOD, MAKE ME BETTER
> PLEASE GOD, HEAR MY PRAYER
> ARE YOU REALLY LISTENING
> ARE YOU REALLY THERE?
>
> I DON'T WANT TO BE AN ANGEL
> I DON'T WANT TO WEAR A CROWN
> IF YOU PUT ME UP ON A BIG WHITE CLOUD
> I'M SURE I'D TUMBLE DOWN
>
> I JUST WANT TO SEE THE GARDEN
> I JUST WANT TO CLIMB THE WALL
> AND I DON'T WANT TO BE AN ANGEL,
> I DON'T WANT TO FLY AT ALL.
>
> PLEASE GOD, MAKE ME STRONGER,
> PLEASE GOD, HEAR MY PRAYER

ARE YOU REALLY LISTENING
ARE YOU REALLY THERE

I DON'T WANT TO WEAR A HALO
I DON'T HAVE CURLY HAIR
AND I DON'T WANT TO PLAY A HARP ALL DAY
NOT EVEN IF YOU'RE THERE!

I JUST WANT TO BE LIKE OTHER BOYS
MAYBE YOU'LL SHOW ME THE WAY—
AND I DON'T WANT TO BE AN ANGEL—
PLEASE—
DON'T TAKE ME AWAY!

(COLIN waits a moment as if listening for an answer, sighs, then lies back. After a moment, MARY enters. He turns away and pulls up the covers.)

MARY. Why didn't you get up?

COLIN *(after a beat)*. I did get up this morning when I thought you were coming. I made them put me back in bed this afternoon. *(Pause.)* Why didn't you come?

MARY. I was working in the garden with Dickon.

COLIN. I won't let that boy come here if you go and stay with him instead of talking to me.

MARY. If you send Dickon away, I'll never come into this room again!

COLIN. I'll make you! They shall drag you in!

MARY. Shall they, Mr. Rajah?! They may drag me in but they can't make me talk when they get me here. I'll sit and clench my teeth. I won't even look at you!

COLIN. You are a selfish thing!

MARY. What are you? Selfish people always say that.

COLIN. I'M not as selfish as you, because I'm always ill, and I'm sure there's a lump coming on my back, and I am going to DIE, besides!

MARY. You are NOT!

COLIN. I AM! You know I am!

MARY. I don't believe it! You just say that to make people sorry.

COLIN. Get out of this room! *(Throws pillow at her.)*

MARY. I'M GOING, AND I WON'T COME BACK!! *(Starts for door.)*

(MEDLOCK, CRAVEN and SERVANTS enter, alarmed.)

MEDLOCK. Good heavens! Good heavens!

CRAVEN *(overlapping)*. What is this? *(To MARY.)* What are you doing in here!? Tell me now, what is this!?

MARY *(at a loss)*. I'm sorry, sir, I—well, we—

COLIN *(in his best Rajah voice)*. Quiet! All of you, Quiet NOW! *(All look at him, amazed.)* This is my cousin, Mary Lennox. I asked her to come and talk to me. *(Looks at MARY. With difficulty.)* I like her. She must come and talk to me whenever I send for her! Whenever!

***Cut to Page 80, cutting Scenes 3 and 4, for shortest version.

CRAVEN *(to MEDLOCK)*. What on earth—

MEDLOCK. I don't know how it happened. There's not a servant on the place tha'd dare talk. They all have their orders. *(SERVANTS nod furiously, and babble.)*

COLIN. Quiet! *(They fall silent.)* Nobody told her anything. She heard me crying and found me herself. I am glad she came. I am better. She made me better. She sang to me last night and it helped me go to sleep. I was better when I

wakened up. I wanted my breakfast. I want my tea now.
NOW, Medlock!

(MUSIC #17A:"HOW WE LOVE CHILDREN"—
Transition)

*(SERVANTS stifle guffaws as the scrim flies in or we shift
to the Great Hall without center section—just portrait
sides. MEDLOCK stalks to a special DL, followed by CRA-
VEN. We see them argue there a moment, then cross to C
followed U by four PORTRAIT CHILDREN in their
frames. The CHILDREN frame MEDLOCK and CRAVEN
during the scene, and their choreography accents the
adults' staging.)*

***Scene 3 may be cut to shorten Act II or for a one-act
version. If Scene 3 is cut and Scene 4 is played, use Music
#17A or #18A for scene change, and go to page 77. In this
case, during the scene change, MARY should see and
"overhear" MEDLOCK and THE DOCTOR talking furtively in pantomime about "getting rid" of the children.
This sets up dialogue in Scene 4 if Scene 3 is cut.

SCENE THREE

SETTING: *The Parlor without center unit and stairs.*

MEDLOCK *(in a fury)*. OOOOOhhhh! That—that—HORRI-
BLE—that—that—that—OBSTINATE—that that—that—
that—IMPUDENT—that—that—that—that—CHILD!
CRAVEN. And the girl! The girl! Did you see her laughing at
you?

MEDLOCK. At ME? They were laughing at YOU, TOO! All of them!

CRAVEN. It WAS funny, you must admit. The way he lorded it over you. "Don't be silly, Medlock." *(He laughs.)* "I want my breakfast, Medlock! NOW!" *(He laughs. She grabs his ear and his "now" turns to "oww.")*

MEDLOCK. I DID NOT FIND IT HUMOROUS! Ooooh, when I am mistress of Misselthwaite—It's enough to make one feel that children should neither be seen NOR heard—but STRANGLED AT BIRTH.

CRAVEN. Humph. Children. Pah. They're of no consequence to us.

MEDLOCK. No consequence? They are of far too MUCH consequence. They are all that stands between us—and THIS! *(She gestures and twirls grandly, referring to the Manor.)* Two little—little—little—CHILDREN!

CRAVEN *(sotto voce, as SERVANTS pass)*. But we must be careful...

MEDLOCK. —we must still seem to care...

CRAVEN. —still seem to cure...

MEDLOCK. —still seem to love—

BOTH. —THEM! *(Sing.)*

(MUSIC #18: "HOW WE LOVE CHILDREN")

**OH, HOW WE LOVE
REALLY DO LOVE
CHILDREN ONE AND ALL (ONE AND ALL)
IT IS SUCH A SURPRISE
IT BRINGS TEARS TO ONE'S EYES
THAT CHILDREN DON'T LOVE US AT ALL**

(MARY creeps in, above, on the stair.)

CRAVEN.
>YOU TRULY ARE A MARVEL, MRS. MEDLOCK
>HAVING SLAVED YOUR EVERY FINGER TO
>   THE BONE

MEDLOCK.
>OH YES, I TRY TO PLAY MY PART
>AND I CAN SAY WITH ALL MY HEART

>YOU'D THINK I LOVED THE LITTLE DARLINGS
>AS MY OWN

>AND HOW I HATE TO TELL THEM ALL AT
>   CHRISTMAS
>THAT THEY MAY NOT EAT THE CAKE OR
>   SUGAR PLUM
>AND WHEN THEY ASK FOR CANDY CANE
>IT GIVES THEM SUCH A FEARFUL PAIN
>I HAVE TO EAT THE SWEET INSTEAD
>AND SEND THEM PROMPTLY OFF TO BED
>WITHOUT A CRUMB

BOTH.
>OH, HOW WE LOVE, REALLY DO LOVE
>CHILDREN, YOU AND ME
>CAN'T YOU SEE
>THEY'RE LIKE SILVER AND GOLD
>SUCH A TREASURE TO HOLD
>A PLEASURE TO BOUNCE ON OUR KNEE

MEDLOCK.
>YOU'RE SUCH A SPLENDID DOCTOR, DOCTOR
>   CRAVEN.

CRAVEN.
>THANK YOU SO MUCH

MEDLOCK.
>ALWAYS CARING FOR THE ILLS OF LITTLE ONES

CRAVEN.
>WHEN WITH MEASLES THEY ARE CURSED
>OR EVEN MUMPS WHICH ARE THE WORST,
>I SIMPLY LOCK THEM IN A ROOM WITHOUT
>>THE SUN
>AND WHEN THEIR WHOOPING COUGH
>WON'T STOP ITS WHOOPING

MEDLOCK.
>WHAT DO YOU DO?

CRAVEN.
>THERE'S A REMEDY I KNOW
>THAT KNOWS NO FAULTS
>I'VE FOUND THAT MOST OF THOSE DISASTERS
>CAN BE CURED WITH MUSTARD PLASTERS
>BUT THE KIDDIES DO RECOIL
>WHEN I LACE THE CASTOR OIL
>WITH EPSOM SALTS!

MEDLOCK *(spoken)*. Oh, you devil, you!

BOTH.
>OH, HOW WE LOVE, REALLY DO LOVE
>CHILDREN EVERYWHERE
>BE THEY BRITISH OR BOER
>FROM BANGKOK TO JAHORE

MEDLOCK.
> **THEY'RE DELIGHTFUL**

CRAVEN.
> **THEY'RE MARVELOUS**

BOTH.
> **CHILDREN, SCHEMING CHILDREN**
> **WHO NEEDS CHILDREN?**
> **WE'LL DREAM OF GOOD RIDDANCE**
> **TO KIDS, DEAR,—I THINK, DEAR**
> **IT'S CLEAR THAT**
> **YOU KNOW WHAT I MEAN—**
>
> **CHILDREN, FOOLISH CHILDREN**
> **RUTHLESS CHILDREN**
> **THE TRUTH IS, WE DON'T LOVE THESE**
> **CHILDREN**
> **THE FAT OR THE THIN ONES, THE SHORT OR**
> **THE TALL!**
> **WE DON'T LOVE CHILDREN**

(Spoken.)
> **AT ALL!**

(They laugh à la Margaret Hamilton and the lights fade as the scenery changes to Mary's room.)

(MUSIC #18A: "HOW WE LOVE CHILDREN"— Playoff/Transition)

**If Scene 3 is used and Scene 4 is cut, add the following dialogue downstage after applause, with scene change music under, during transition to Colin's room.

(NURSE enters.)

NURSE. Beggin' your pardon, sir, madam—but it's Master Colin. He's havin' what the doctor calls hysterics. And Miss Mary is havin' them with him! *(They move to Colin's room.)*

**The next scene may be cut to shorten Act II, or for a one-act version. Continue here if Scene 3 is cut.

SCENE FOUR

SETTING: *Mary's room, or a hallway (downstage, in one).*

MARTHA. Good riddance?

MARY. That's what they were saying—good riddance to the children—and I think they were talking about Colin as well as me! Can they get rid of me, Martha? Are they going to send me away—?

MARTHA. Now, tha's all upset over nothin, I'm sure—

MARY. But Colin is angry at me, too—maybe he told them to send me away—!

MARTHA. But Colin likes you! He said he wants you to visit—

MARY. He just said that because Medlock and everyone was there. We had a fight and he said I was selfish and told me to get out—and I said HE'S selfish and I'd never come back. *(She dissolves in tears.)*

MARTHA. Here, now! Here! Enough of this rainstorm and cloudy face! You know what? Colin IS selfish, and tha' might be the only one who can tell him so. The rest of us are all afraid of him. Come to the window. Can tha' see that bit o' blue sky peekin' through the clouds? It's big enough to make a sailor suit, and tha' knows what that means! *(MARTHA sings.)*

(MUSIC #19: "ONE PATCH OF BLUE")

WITH ONE PATCH OF BLUE
JUST ONE GLIMPSE OF SKY
AND A STAR SHINING THROUGH
MAKE A WISH AND WISH IT TRUE

ONE RAINBOW HIGH
WILL RISE OVER YOU
AS THE CLOUDS ROLL BY
YOU CAN WISH YOUR DREAMS COME TRUE
YOU MUST WAIT, YOU MUST WAIT
WHILE THOSE THOUSANDS OF RAINDROPS
  KEEP FALLING

THEY WILL SOON STOP,
AND THE LAST DROP
SAYS GET READY—GET SET TO START WISHING

ON THAT ONE PATCH OF BLUE
THAT ONE GLIMPSE OF SKY
AND A STAR SHINING THROUGH
MAKE A WISH—AND WISH IT TRUE
MAKE A WISH, AND WISH IT TRUE

(NURSE enters.)

NURSE. Miss Mary—Martha—beggin' your pardon, but it's Master Colin—*(COLIN is heard wailing).* He's havin' one of those tantrums the doctor calls hysterics! *(COLIN is heard, louder.)* I don't know what to do—I can't bear it!

MARY. He ought to be stopped! Somebody ought to just make him stop!

NURSE. He'll do himself harm. He's worked himself into hysterics. No one can do anything with him. You come and try, like a good child. He likes you.

MARY *(with a stamp of her foot)*. He turned me out of the room this morning.

NURSE. That's right! You're in the right humor! You go and scold him. Go, child, as quick as you can!

(MARY exits, followed by MARTHA, and the scenery changes as the SERVANTS sing.)

(MUSIC #19A: "ANY MINUTE NOW"—Reprise)

SERVANTS.
>   **MISS MARY WILL BE COMIN'**
>   **ANY MINUTE NOW**
>   **TO STOP THE BOY'S TANTRUMMING**
>   **ANY MINUTE NOW**

(The following is spoken over the continuing instrumental.)

MEDLOCK. What is this? What on earth?

MAID. They're going for Miss Mary, mum, to calm him down.

MEDLOCK. Miss Mary! Indeed not! That girl will not set foot in this room!

SERVANTS *(singing).*
> **ANY MINUTE, THE CARRIAGE WILL BE
> COMIN', COMIN', COMIN', COMIN', COMIN',
> COMIN'
> ANY MINUTE NOW.**

SCENE FIVE

***Continue here from page 72 or 77 for one-act version or scenes should be cut.

(MARY bolts toward Colin, past MEDLOCK.)

MARY *(to COLIN).* You STOP! YOU STOP! I hate you! Everybody hates you! I wish everybody would run out of the house *(She chases SERVANTS out.)* and let you scream yourself to death!

COLIN. I can't stop! I can't!

MARY. Yes you can! Half that ails you is hysterics and temper—just hysterics—hysterics!—hysterics! *(The last repeat drives MEDLOCK, who had crept forward, back away.)*

COLIN. I felt the lump—I felt it! I shall have a hump on my back when I die *(He writhes and moans.)*

MARY. You didn't feel a lump! If you did it was only a hysterical lump! There's nothing the matter with your horrid back. Turn over and let me look at it! Nurse, come here and show me his back this minute! *(The NURSE comes forward, and pulls COLIN's pajama top up. MARY inspects his back like a great surgeon.)* There's not a single lump there! There's not a lump as big as a pin! If you ever say there is again, I shall laugh!

NURSE. I—I didn't know that he thought he had a lump on his spine. His back is weak because he won't try to sit up. I could have told him there was no lump there.

COLIN *(turning to NURSE)*. Could you?

NURSE. Yes, sir.

MARY. There!

COLIN *(to NURSE again)*. Do you think—I could—live to grow up?

NURSE. You probably will if you do not give way to your temper, and eat what you are served, and get some exercise and fresh air.

COLIN *(extending a hand to MARY)*. I'll go out with you, Mary. I'd like to go outside if we can find the—*(Pause.)* If we can find Dickon to push my chair. I do so want to see Dickon and the fox and the crow—

MARY. You'll see them soon enough. *(Lies him back.)* But now you must get your rest or you'll be too fretful to plan our going out tomorrow—

MEDLOCK. Going out—really!

MARY. Shhh!—*(Waves MEDLOCK away, gestures to NURSE to usher the others out.)*—because you must be fresh and rested for us to go out into the fresh air like the nurse suggested—perhaps into the gardens, where Ben Weatherstaff works—

COLIN. Oh, could we, really?

MARY. Oh, I'm sure Mrs. Medlock and Doctor Craven will understand—a growing boy needs fresh air and exercise and a good breakfast to strengthen his back. *(To MEDLOCK.)* Doesn't he? *(MEDLOCK, beaten, nods.)* And Martha will ask Dickon to come help us, won't you, Martha. Now, would you like me to sing to you so you can sleep? *(The others leave. MARTHA stays in the "hallway" nearby.)*

COLIN. Oh, yes. I shall go to sleep in a minute—but Mary, tell me, what do you imagine the secret garden looks like inside? I'm sure it will make me go to sleep, and dream, and dream...

MARY. Yes, of course I will. Now, close your eyes. *(He lies back, and closes them. MARTHA stands nearby, listening. She hums, then aahs, then sings.)*

(MUSIC #20: "SOMETHING SPECIAL"—Reprise)

MARY. I think the garden has grown all into a lovely tangle. I think the roses have climbed until they hang from the branches and walls. And when the summer comes there will be curtains and fountains of roses.

MARTHA.
> NOW I LAY ME DOWN TO SLEEP, AND THANK
> THEE FOR THIS DAY
> AND ONE THING'S CERTAIN, VERY CERTAIN
> SOMETHING SPECIAL HAPPENS THAT WAY

(Lights fade.)

SCENE SIX

SETTING: *In front of the scrim, then Colin's bedroom.*

MEDLOCK *(to DR. CRAVEN)*. How is he? You'll scarcely believe your eyes. That plain-faced sour girl that's almost as bad as himself has just BEWITCHED him. She just flew at him like a little cat last night, and stamped her feet, and ORDERED him to stop screaming, AND shooed the rest of us out of the room—and somehow she startled him so that

he DID stop! And this morning—Well, just come in and
see—*(DR. CRAVEN and MEDLOCK exit.)*

*(The scrim fades through. DICKON, MARTHA, MARY—
and DICKON's MENAGERIE are in the room with
COLIN, and all are singing. The CROW is on the floor at
the foot of the bed, and chases MEDLOCK away several
times during the scene.)*

(MUSIC #21: "YOUR BEST FOOT"—Reprise)

DICKON, MARTHA, MARY, COLIN & ANIMALS.
    SO KEEP YOUR CHIN UP
    AND EVEN A GRIN UP YOUR SLEEVE
    WILL SHOW THEM WHO'S WHO
    WITH ONE LITTLE LEFT FOOT
    YOU'LL BE ON YOUR BEST FOOT
    AND THAT'S THE BEST—YOU CAN DOOO—

(CRAVEN and MEDLOCK stride in.)

CRAVEN. I am sorry to hear you were ill last night, my boy.
COLIN. I'm better now, much better.
MEDLOCK *(approaching bed)*. That's very good, dear, but—
CROW *(at MEDLOCK)*. Caw! Caw!
COLIN. I'm going out in my chair this afternoon. I want
    some fresh air.
CRAVEN *(sits on the bed, takes his pulse)*. You must be very
    careful not to tire yourself— *(The FOX jumps on the bed
    near CRAVEN, startling him.)*
COLIN. Fresh air won't tire me.
CRAVEN. I thought you didn't like fresh air—

COLIN. I don't when I am by myself, but my cousin is going out with me, and also Dickon and his friends—

MEDLOCK *(moving nearer).* —and the nurse, of course—

CROW. Caw! Caw! Caw! *(MEDLOCK moves away, across the room.)*

COLIN. No, I will not have the nurse. *(MEDLOCK and CRAVEN look at each other.)* My cousin knows how to take care of me. I am always better when she is with me. She made me better last night. And Dickon will push my carriage. He is an animal charmer, and these are his friends.

MARY. He's trusty, Dickon is. He's the trustiest lad i' Yorkshire.

MEDLOCK. I hope the animals will not—AH—BITE, Master Colin—

COLIN. Charmers' animals never bite *(The FOX moves a bit toward MEDLOCK who withdraws.)*

MARY. There are snake charmers in India, and they can put their snakes' heads in their mouths. *(The FOX jumps, MEDLOCK screams.)*

CRAVEN *(checking COLIN's pulse).* You are evidently better, but you must remember—*(The two SQUIRRELS begin to climb around on CRAVEN as COLIN speaks the following, one climbing up to his head; the FOX and/or the CROW move toward a wary MEDLOCK.)*

COLIN. I don't want to remember. When I lie by myself and remember I have pains everywhere and I think of things that make me scream because I hate them so. It is because my cousin makes me forget that she makes me better.

MEDLOCK. But Master Colin, you really should not—

CROW. Caw! Caw!

COLIN. I am going out in my chair this afternoon. If the fresh air agrees with me, I may go out every day. When I go, none of the gardeners or anyone else is to be anywhere near the Long Walk and the gazebo by the garden walls. Everyone is to keep away until I send word that they may go back to their work.

CRAVEN. But, sir—

COLIN. Mary, what is that thing you say in India when you have finished talking and want people to go?

MARY. You say, "You have my permission to go."

COLIN. You have my permission to go, Medlock, Doctor. But remember my instructions!

CROW (*as MEDLOCK and CRAVEN move D, preparing to exit*). CAW!

CRAVEN. I must send a note to Archie in Italy—he's at Lake Como—he'll restore our authority!

MEDLOCK. No, you fool! Leave Archie where he is! Gone! And living in the past!

CROW. CAW! CAW! CAW! CAW! CAW! (*MEDLOCK and CRAVEN flee.*)

(*The scrim flies in as the bedroom darkens. We see a brief interlude of flirtation between DR. CRAVEN and a MAID, who then is beckoned and chased off by MEDLOCK. The music changes, and MARTHA enters.*)

SCENE SEVEN

SETTING: *In front of scrim, then in garden.*

MARTHA, out walking, crosses the stage, observing the world around her. As she speaks, through the scrim we see a little procession—MARY, COLIN in his chair, and DICKON pushing, with the ANIMALS in tow—making its way from U down toward the gazebo, and then to the se-

cret door. The CHILDREN we see are "doubles" part of the time, to enable us to see them approach the Secret Garden, and then move our point of view inside the garden to see them enter.

("MUSIC #22: "MAGIC")

MARTHA. One o' the strange things about livin' in the world is that now an' then we're quite sure we will live forever. We know it sometimes at dawn as the pale sky slowly changes and tha' heart stands still at the strange majesty of the risin' o' the sun. And we know it standin' in a wood at sunset, when the mysterious deep gold stillness slants through the branches. Then sometimes the immense quiet of the dark blue at night makes us sure—with millions of stars waitin' and watchin'. And sometimes we know it from a look in someone's eyes.

(The CHILDREN emerge into the Secret Garden, perhaps welcomed by LILIAN, who they do not see, as MARTHA sings.)

**THERE LIES A MAGIC PLACE
WHERE MARIGOLDS EMBRACE
AND MORNING SONGBIRDS SOAR
A GARDEN OF SURPRISE
RIGHT BEFORE OUR EYES
THAT GROWNUPS JUST IGNORE**
(They explore and celebrate.)
**WE WANDER THROUGH A MAZE
REGRETTING YESTERDAYS
AND MISS THE GLOWING ROSE
WHEN FROM THE VERY START**

THE CHILDISH HEART CAN TELL YOU
HOW THE FLOWER GROWS

EACH BRIGHT AND MAGIC MORN
A MIRACLE IS BORN
AND LOVE APPEARS TO WARM THE SKY
(LILIAN approaches Colin's chair, and he basks in the warming sun of her love.)
IT 'S LOVE THAT HAS FOUND US
ITS MAGIC ASTOUNDS US
RIGHT HERE BEFORE OUR EYES

EACH BRIGHT AND MAGIC MORN
A MIRACLE IS BORN
AND LOVE APPEARS TO WARM THE SKY
(LILIAN dances, causing petals to fall from a tree.)
IT'S LOVE THAT HAS FOUND US
ITS MAGIC ASTOUNDS US
RIGHT HERE BEFORE OUR EYES
(The scrim flies at the end of the song, MARTHA disappears.)

SCENE EIGHT

SETTING: *Inside the Secret Garden.*

COLIN, DICKON and MARY stop for a moment just to smell the air and feel the sun.

COLIN. I wonder if we shall see the robin?
DICKON. Look! There he is—he's been foragin' for his dinner!
COLIN. And the fox—where is he?

DICKON. Captain? Master Colin's askin' for ye—

(The FOX appears.)

COLIN. I don't want this afternoon to go. But I shall come
back tomorrow, and the day after, and the day after...

MARY. You'll get plenty of fresh air, won't you?

COLIN. I'm going to get nothing else! I've seen the spring
and now I'm going to see the summer! I'm going to see
everything grow here! I'm going to grow here myself.

DICKON. That tha' will. Us'll have thee walkin' about here
and diggin' same as other folk afore long.

COLIN. Walk! And dig? Shall I?

DICKON. For sure tha' will. Tha'—tha's got legs o' thine
own, same as other folks.

COLIN. Nothing really ails them. But they are so thin and
weak. They shake so that I'm afraid to try and stand on
them.

DICKON. When tha' stops bein' afraid tha'lt stand on them.
And tha'lt stop being afraid in a bit.

COLIN. I shall? *(To the LAMB.)* I shall! *(Pause. He rocks the
LAMB.)* Who is that man? *(Pointing at a head sticking
over the wall.)*

MARY. Look!

(BEN is there.)

BEN. If I wasn't a bachelor, and tha' were my daughter, I'd
give thee a hidin'! However did tha' get in here—!

MARY. Ben Weatherstaff, the robin showed me the way—

BEN. Tha' young bad 'un! Layin' tha' badness on a robin—

MARY. The robin showed me! He didn't know he was doing
it, but he did—

COLIN. Do you know who I am? Answer!

BEN. Who tha' art? Aye, that I do—with tha' mother's eyes starin' at me out o' tha' face. Lord knows how tha' come here, but tha' are th' poor cripple.

COLIN. I'm not a cripple! I'm not.

MARY (*overlapping*). He's not! He's not got a lump as big as a pin.

BEN. Tha'—tha' hasn't got a crooked back?

COLIN. No!

BEN. Tha' hasn't got crooked legs?

COLIN (*to DICKON*). Come here! (*DICKON runs to him as COLIN tears the blankets off his lap.*) Come here this minute! I'll show you! (*He begins to try to stand.*) You get down from that ladder and go out to the gazebo and Miss Mary will meet you and bring you here. Now you will have to be in on the secret. Be quick!

BEN (*getting down*). Eh, lad! Eh, my lad! Yes sir! Yes sir! (*MARY runs to the door and out.*)

COLIN (*to DICKON*). I can stand. I can do it! I'm not a cripple! (*He struggles to stand, fails.*)

DICKON (*surging, helping him*). I told thee tha' could as soon as tha' stopped bein' afraid, and tha's stopped!

COLIN. Yes, I've stopped being afraid. (*Pause.*) I'm feeling stronger! Are you making magic? (*Another effort, closer to success.*)

DICKON. Tha's makin' magic thysel'! It's same magic as made these 'ere crocus work out of the earth. Come now, magic!

(*MARY and BEN rush in.*)

COLIN. Aye. I AM MAKING MAGIC! I CAN STAND! I CAN DO IT! UP—

MARY. You can do it. You can do it!

COLIN. I can DO it! I CAN DO IT! *(He stands, ALL fall silent. To BEN.)* Look at me! Look at me all over! Am I a hunchback?! Have I got crooked legs?! Who says so?!

BEN. Lots o' fools! The world's full o' jackasses brayin', an' they never bray nowt but lies! When I see'd thee put thy legs on the gound, I know'd tha' was all right. An' she'd have loved it happenin' here—in her garden.

COLIN. Her garden?

BEN. Tha' mother.

COLIN. My mother? This was her garden?

BEN. Aye. She were so fond of it, your mother. And she was such a prettly young thing. She says to me once, "Ben," says she, laughin'—"If ever I'm ill, or go away, you must take care o' my roses."

COLIN. Her roses. Her garden. It's my garden now. I am fond of it. I shall come here every day! Everybody thought I was going to die. But I'm not! I shall live forever!

***This song may be cut for one-act or shorter version. If this is done, all cheer COLIN at end of scene.

(MUSIC #23: "I SHALL LIVE FOREVER")

(COLIN struggles to his feet, takes a rose from BEN, and plants it with DICKON's help. COLIN then sings.)

    I SHALL LIVE FOREVER
    AND I'LL GROW TALL AND WELL
    RACES I'LL BE WINNING
    LIKE A TOP I WILL BE SPINNING
    I'LL DO ALMOST ANYTHING,
    THE STORIES THEY WILL TELL

I SHALL WALK THE HEATHER
WITH DICKON BY MY SIDE
AND WHEN MY FATHER SEES ME ONCE AGAIN

COLIN & ALL.
HIS SMILE WILL BE
HIS SMILE WILL BE
HIS SMILE WILL BE
A FATHER'S SMILE OF PRIDE
(Lights darken quickly on applause. The scrim falls to end the scene, as a projection comes onto the scrim: Lake Como, Italy.)

SCENE NINE

SETTING: *Downstage right a WAITER places a round table and a chair. ARCHIE enters and speaks to the WAITER.*

(MUSIC #24: "MY FAVORITE SONG")

ARCHIE. Would you be kind enough to ask the orchestra to play those melodies again?

WAITER. Any particular one, sir?

ARCHIE. No, no, any of them will do *(The WAITER goes).* Any of them and none of them will do. *(Sings.)*
IF YOU PLAY ME MY FAVORITE SONG
PLAY EVERY NOTE SHE SANG FOR ME
I'LL ONLY HEAR
A REVERIE PLAY ON

IF YOU PLAY ME MY FAVORITE WALTZ
PLAY EVERY STEP SHE DANCED WITH ME

I'LL ONLY HEAR
A RHAPSODY PLAY ON

PLAY ME THE MOUNTAINS RINGING
RIVERS SINGING
OCEANS ROARING,
FOUNTAINS SOARING
OVERFLOWING, FILLING MY LIFE
WITH A SYMPHONY

IF YOU PLAY ME MY FAVORITE TUNE
PLAY EVERY NOTE SO SWEET AND CLEAR
I'LL ONLY HEAR
A MEMORY PLAY ON

(An instrumental break, during which we see LILIAN come out of the portrait to speak to ARCHIE, and then dance with "YOUNG ARCHIE" U of the scrim. The following is spoken over continuing instrumental.)

LILIAN *(reverb)*. Archie—Archie—come back, Archie—

ARCHIE. Lilian—where are you—where ARE YOU!

LILIAN. In the garden...the garden...*(She dances with YOUNG ARCHIE.)*

ARCHIE. Lilian!—*(He is strengthened, revived by her presence. Sings.)*
    PLAY ME THE MOUNTAINS RINGING,
    RIVERS SINGING, OCEANS ROARING
    FOUNTAINS SOARING, OVERFLOWING
    FILLING MY LIFE WITH A SYMPHONY

IF YOU PLAY ME MY FAVORITE TUNE
PLAY EVERY NOTE SO SWEET AND CLEAR
I'LL ONLY HEAR A MEMORY PLAY ON

(WAITER enters. The following is spoken over instrumental:)

(MUSIC #24, Section B)

WAITER. There's a letter for you, sir. *(Leaves it on the table and goes.)*

ARCHIE *(opens letter and begins to read).* "Dear sir, please forgive me for writing to you, sir, but things are happening…"

(MARTHA has entered DL, and continues the letter.)

MARTHA. "…but things are happening at Misselthwaite that you should know about. You must come home, sir—you must! Your respectful servant, Martha Sowerby." *(LILIAN dances joyously in her garden as ARCHIE feels hope again.)*

ARCHIE.
NIGHT AFTER NIGHT I'VE BEEN DREAMING
DREAMS
LOVELY DREAMS OF THOSE HAPPY DAYS I
LEFT BEHIND

ARCHIE & MARTHA.
ON MY WINGS

ARCHIE.
MAGIC WINGS,

    GLIDING MOONBEAMS
    I'LL BE HOME, HOME AGAIN

MARTHA.
    FLYING HOME

BOTH.
    HOME AGAIN.

ARCHIE.
    ON WINGS,

MARTHA.
    MAGIC WINGS

ARCHIE.
    RIDING RAINBOWS
    I'LL BE HOME

MARTHA.
    FLYING HOME

BOTH
    ON MY OWN MAGIC WINGS

(ARCHIE looks at the letter as, behind the scrim, the dancers embrace at the end of the instrumental tag. On applause, the lights change again, and grows darker behind the scrim, and LILIAN returns to her garden. LILIAN whispers, reverb, over music tag.)

(MUSIC #24A: "MY FAVORITE SONG"—Playoff)

SCENE TEN

SETTING: *In the Secret Garden. The garden has bloomed further, with additional plants and sections coming into their "summer" look, but the main "summer" scenery is not in yet.*

MARY, COLIN and DICKON are discovered.

MARY. Be careful, Colin—

COLIN. I will—I know—

DICKON. It's bein' too careful has kept him pale and weak. This week here in the garden has made him strong—

COLIN. I am stronger—just from coming here every day, and digging, and walking—there is something special here. It's almost magical—*(He extends his arms, as if to feel the magic.)*—good magic, you know, Mary? There's magic here. I'm sure of it.

MARY *(extending her arms)*. So am I.

(DICKON extends his arms, and all stand still a moment, arms out, sensing the magic, as BEN enters.)

BEN. Eh, 'tis a field of scarecrows, I see.

DICKON *(a big whisper)*. Shhh! Ben! We're waiting for the magic!

MARY. We're trying to feel the magic working—the magic here that makes Colin stronger. *(MARY assumes the "scarecrow" again, as does DICKON.)*

BEN *(a whisper)*. Oh, aye, the magic—*(BEN becomes a scarecrow.)* The magic!

COLIN. When I grow up I am going to make great scientific discoveries, and I am going to begin now with an experiment about magic. Every morning and evening I am going to say "Magic is in me! Magic is making me well! I am going to be as strong as Dickon, as strong as Dickon." And you must all do it too. Will you help, Ben Weatherstaff?

BEN. Aye, aye, sir!

COLIN. Then we must sit in a circle!

(COLIN leads them into formation. Once DICKON sits, the ANIMALS come and sit near the circle, joining them.)

COLIN. The creatures have come. They want to help us. Now we will begin. Shall we sway backward and forward, Mary, like dervishes?

BEN *(a bit spooked by all this)*. I canna' do no swayin' back'ard. I've got the rheumatics.

COLIN. The magic will take them away. But we won't sway until it has done it. We will only chant. *(He takes a breath to chant.)* Then I will chant.

(MUSIC #25: "WEAVE A SPELL")

DICKON. And I will play! *("WEAVE A SPELL"—Intro, as if played on the recorder by DICKON, then picked up by the orchestra. Chanted in rhythm.)*

COLIN.
> **THE SUN IS SHINING**
> **THE SUN IS SHINING**
> **THAT IS THE MAGIC**

ALL.
> **THAT IS THE MAGIC**

COLIN.
>
> **THE FLOWERS ARE GROWING**
>
> **THE ROOTS ARE STIRRING**
> **THAT IS THE MAGIC**
>
> **BEING ALIVE IS THE MAGIC**
> **BEING STRONG IS THE MAGIC**
>
> **THE MAGIC IS IN ME!**

ALL.
>
> **THE MAGIC IS IN ME**

COLIN.
>
> **THE MAGIC IS IN ME**

ALL.
>
> **THE MAGIC IS IN ME**

COLIN.
>
> **MAGIC, MAGIC**
> **COME AND HELP!**

ALL.
>
> **MAGIC, MAGIC,**
> **COME AND HELP!**
>
> *(COLIN begins to lead a procession around the garden, following the beckoning LILIAN without really knowing it, but following SOMETHING that draws him.)*

DICKON *(sings).*
>
> **WEAVE A SPELL, MAGIC SPELL, TURN AND SPIN**

ALL.
> WEAVE A SPELL, YOU CAN TELL, WHEN YOU'RE IN
> A LOVELY MAGIC LAND, WHERE YOUR WISHES
>   ALL COME TRUE
> AND YOU CAN FEEL THE MAGIC IN YOU
> *(Instrumental bridge; the CHILDREN's actions [slow motion?] and the lighting changes suggesting the passage of time. COLIN grows stronger, even powerful as he comes forward to sing. Jackets and sweaters have come off, sleeves rolled up.)*

COLIN.
> WEAVE A SPELL, MAGIC SPELL, TURN AND SPIN

ALL.
> WEAVE A SPELL, YOU CAN TELL, WHEN WE'RE IN
> A LOVELY MAGIC LAND, WHERE YOUR WISHES
>   ALL COME TRUE
> *(Retard last line.)*
> AND WE CAN SEE WHAT MAGIC CAN DO
> AND WE CAN SEE WHAT MAGIC CAN DO!
> *(MUSIC under. MARY and DICKON start to dig and garden. COLIN strides forward, robust and strong.)*

COLIN. Mary! Dickon! Just look at me! *(They do.)* Do you remember that first morning when you brought me in here?

DICKON. Aye, that we do. *(MARY nods).*

COLIN *(to BEN, DICKON and MARY).* Just this minute, all at once I remembered myself—when I looked at my hand digging with the trowel—and I had to stand up on my feet to see if it was real—and it IS REAL! I'M WELL! I'M WELL! I FEEL AS IF I MIGHT SHOUT OUT SOMETHING THANKFUL, JOYFUL!

(MUSIC #26: "DOXOLOGY")

BEN (*watching, moved*). Aye—something thankful...
  (*Sings a capella.*)
    PRAISE GOD FROM WHOM ALL BLESSINGS FLOW
    PRAISE HIM ALL CREATURES HERE BELOW...

COLIN. What is that?
MARY. The doxology. We sing it in church
COLIN. I've never been to church. I was always too ill—

BEN, MARY & DICKON.
    PRAISE HIM ABOVE YE HEAVENLY HOST—

BEN.
    PRAISE FATHER, SON, AND HOLY GHOST
  (*A pipe organ is heard—the organ from the funeral at the
  start of the play. LILIAN gestures, and the sun streams
  down powerfully on COLIN.*)

COLIN. The magic—I feel the magic—more than ever before.
    PRAISE GOD FROM WHOM ALL BLESSINGS FLOW

COLIN & LILIAN.
    PRAISE HIM ALL CREATURES HERE BELOW

ALL.
    PRAISE HIM ABOVE THE HEAVENLY HOST

  (*ARCHIE enters the garden at the back, with MARTHA.
  Other SERVANTS are seen outside, through the door.*)

ALL.

PRAISE FATHER—
(All turn to ARCHIE, as LILIAN draws ARCHIE forward.)
PRAISE FATHER,
(LILIAN draws FATHER and SON together in an embrace.)
PRAISE FATHER, SON,
AND HOLY GHOST

(LILIAN embraces them without touching. ARCHIE steps back from the embrace, to look at COLIN, as the garden erupts with SERVANTS. Even MEDLOCK and CRAVEN follow in, timidly, at rear.)

COLIN. Father! I'm Colin! You can't believe it! *(They embrace again—ALL crowd around them; MARY is swept aside for a moment.)* It was the garden that did it! And Mary, and Dickon, and the creatures, and magic—

ARCHIE. And Lillian—!

BEN. And the Good Lord Himself, I'd say, sir.

MEDLOCK. But Miss Mary, sir—it was mostly Miss Mary. We didn't help the boy. We should have been able to, Doctor Craven and I—but we didn't, sorry, sir. But Mary did.

ARCHIE. Wait, Mrs. Medlock, Richard—Thank you for your honesty. You were filled with the same darkness that consumed me for so long. I will see that you each have a cottage of you own from now on—if you wish. *(MEDLOCK embraces him, and moves to CRAVEN. LILIAN again turns ARCHIE to MARY.)* Thank you, Mary.

MARY *(shyly, formal like him)*. Thank you, sir. For letting me come stay with you. And Colin. And everyone. *(ARCHIE's reserve dissolves; he drops to his knees and opens his arms to her, and she flies to his embrace. After a beat, COLIN joins them.)*

ARCHIE *(standing, arms around COLIN and MARY).* Well, Weatherstaff—what do you make of this, then. Haven't I a fine son?

BEN. That ye have, sir—but ye'v a lot to thank Miss Mary for.

MARY. And the garden. It was really the garden. And Dickon. And Ben! And Martha! Oh, it was everyone! EVERYONE!

(MUSIC #27: "FINALE")

ALL.
> SO KEEP YOUR CHIN UP
> AND EVEN A GRIN UP YOUR SLEEVE
> WILL SHOW THEM WHO'S WHO
> AND ONE LITTLE LEFT FOOT
> WILL LEAD TO THE NEXT FOOT
> AND THAT'S THE BEST YOU CAN DO

(MARY dashes to embrace MARTHA.)

MARTHA.
> WHEN YOU HEAR A ROBIN SING
> SOMETHING SPECIAL HAPPENS WHEN A ROBIN SINGS.

ARCHIE.
> AND WHEN YOU SEE LILACS BLOOM IN SPRING

ARCHIE & MARTHA.
> ALL THE WORLD'S BEEN SLEEPING IN ITS COZY BED
> THEN SOMETHING SPECIAL HAPPENS TO WAKE UP ITS SLEEPY HEAD

ALL.

> AND LATE AT NIGHT WHEN YOU'RE ALONE
> SOMETHING SPECIAL HAPPENS SO YOU'RE
>   NOT ALONE
> JUST CLOSE YOUR EYES, YOUR HEART KNOWS
>   WHAT TO SAY
> NOW I LAY ME DOWN TO SLEEP, AND THANK
>   THEE FOR THIS DAY
>
> AND ONE THING'S CERTAIN
> VERY CERTAIN
> SOMETHING SPECIAL HAPPENS
> THAT WAY
>   THE END

(MUSIC #28: "BOWS")

(For bows, reprise "SOMETHING SPECIAL" again, be-ginning at meas. 53; Ensemble singing at "And late at night.")

ALL.

> AND LATE AT NIGHT WHEN YOU'RE ALONE
> SOMETHING SPECIAL HAPPENS SO YOU'RE
>   NOT ALONE
> JUST CLOSE YOUR EYES, YOUR HEART
>   KNOWS WHAT TO SAY
> NOW I LAY ME DOWN TO SLEEP, AND THANK
>   THEE FOR THIS DAY
> AND ONE THING'S CERTAIN
> VERY CERTAIN
> SOMETHING SPECIAL HAPPENS
> THAT WAY
>   END OF CURTAIN CALL

***Optional insert (see page 56)

SCENE NINE-B

SETTING: *Still in the Great Hall.*

MEDLOCK. That girl is becoming more and more impossible! And as for Archie...

CRAVEN. You must be patient! Remember, one day things will be different!

MEDLOCK. Different! It's easy for you to say that! It's always ME that is left to deal with HIS problems—whatever they are! Perhaps, one day things will be different!

(MUSIC #12B: "TRADITIONS")

MEDLOCK.
ONE HUNDRED YEARS, ONE HUNDRED WAYS
    TO SERVE THE TRADITIONS WE KNOW.
AND I'M TIRED OF—
"BRING ME THE PAPERS!

CRAVEN *(simultaneously).*
RING FOR THE FOOTMAN!"

MEDLOCK.
"SEND FOR MY CARRIAGE, I'M LEAVING FOR
    PARIS
AND CATCHING THE BOAT TRAIN—YOU'LL
    SEE ME IN PERHAPS A MONTH,"

CRAVEN.
"MAYBE TWO"

MEDLOCK.
AND I'VE NEVER SEEN PARIS—WILL I EVER
SEE PARIS?

CRAVEN.
DOES IT SPARKLE LIKE A DIAMOND, DOES IT
GLISTEN, DOES IT SHINE

MEDLOCK.
DO THE RUBIES GROW LIKE ROSES,

BOTH.
DO THE RIVERS FLOW WITH WINE

MEDLOCK.
AND I'D LIKE TO SEE PARIS,

BOTH.
I'D LIKE IT JUST FINE

MEDLOCK.
I'LL HAVE RUBIES BIG AS ROSES, DRINK
FROM RIVERS FILLED
WITH ONE THOUSAND YEARS OF TRADITION
AND A THOUSAND AND ONE WAYS TO LIVE

CRAVEN.
I'LL RING FOR THE FOOTMAN,

MEDLOCK *(spoken)*. No!

CRAVEN.
SEND FOR THE PAPERS,

MEDLOCK *(spoken).* No!
  (Sings.)
    ORDER MY CARRIAGE WHEN I'M GOING TO
      PARIS, AND CATCHING THE BOAT TRAIN,

BOTH.
    WE'LL LEAVE IN A MONTH
    MAYBE TWO, MAYBE NOT
    IF TRADITIONS DON'T CHANGE IN THESE ONE
      HUNDRED ROOMS—

MEDLOCK.
    FOR THE NEXT HUNDRED YEARS.

CRAVEN *(echoes).*
    NEXT HUNDRED YEARS

BOTH.
    THEN I'LL BE LEAVING
    SOON—!

Musical Selections

ACT ONE

ACT TWO

DIRECTOR'S NOTES

DIRECTOR'S NOTES

DIRECTOR'S NOTES